A Mark Dahle Portfolio

The Birth Of Aesop

A Little Luck
Changes Everything

(Fables About Aesop #2)

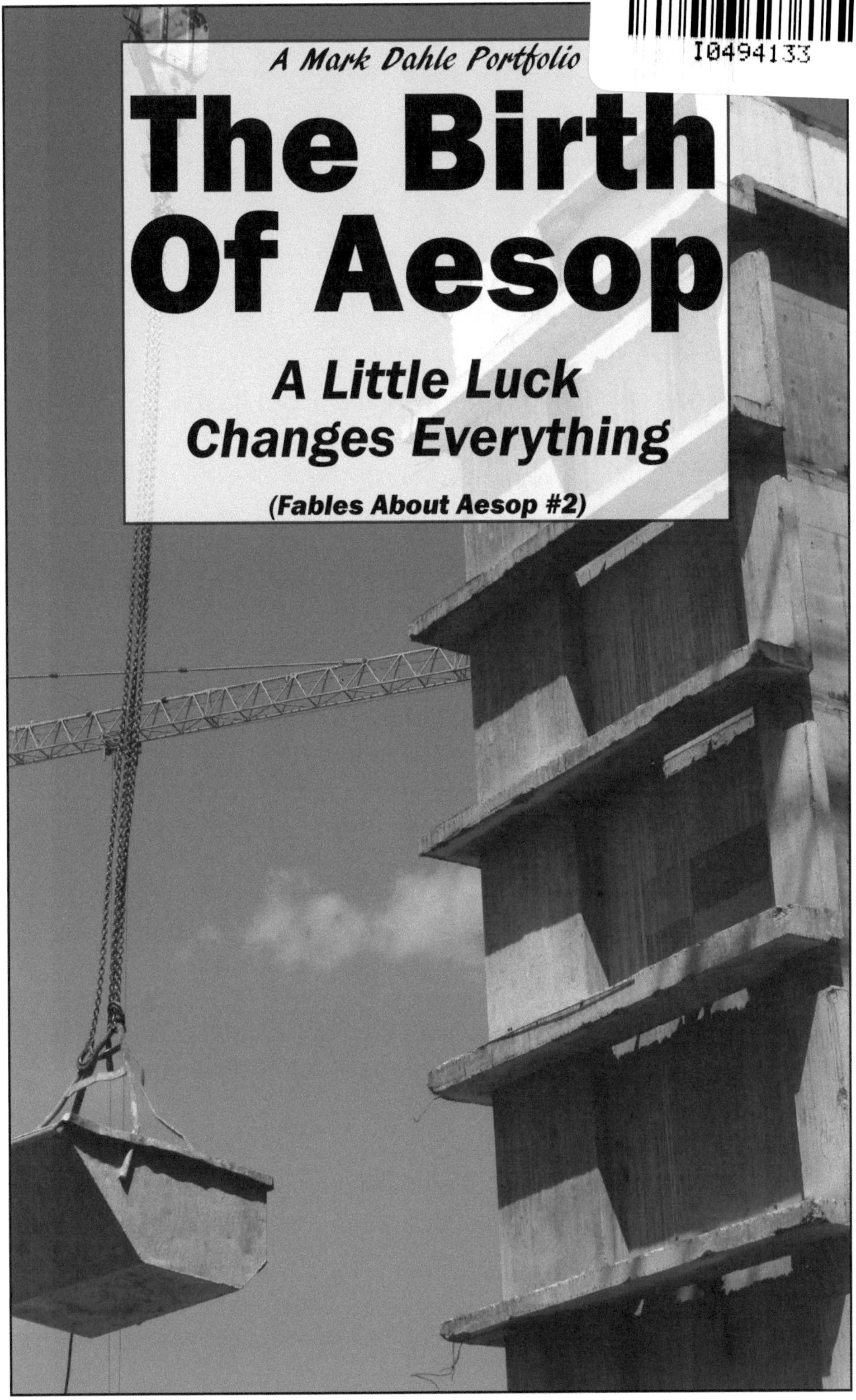

Mark Dahle has written many great fables about Aesop.
This is #2.

~ ~ ~

Mark Dahle Portfolios can be read in a few minutes and enjoyed for a lifetime.

Unlike many picture books, the text is not related to the beautiful painting at the right and the photographs that follow. This might seem a little weird at first. One thing that helps is to order more portfolios until you get used to it. In the meantime, feel free to draw your own pictures of Aesop growing up if you like.

This portfolio includes a photo of a brilliant 36 x 24 inch painting (at the right), twenty-six beautiful pictures from Freiburg, Germany, and a story about Aesop's birth.

Photographs in this book are available in very limited editions. See http://www.MarkDahle.com for more information and for previews of upcoming portfolios.

We do our best to create portfolios free of editing mistakes. But it's hard to catch everything. We reward people who report errors in any Mark Dahle portfolio. For details see MarkDahle.com/Typos.html or send an email to MarkDahle@aol.com with the subject line "Typos." Thanks!

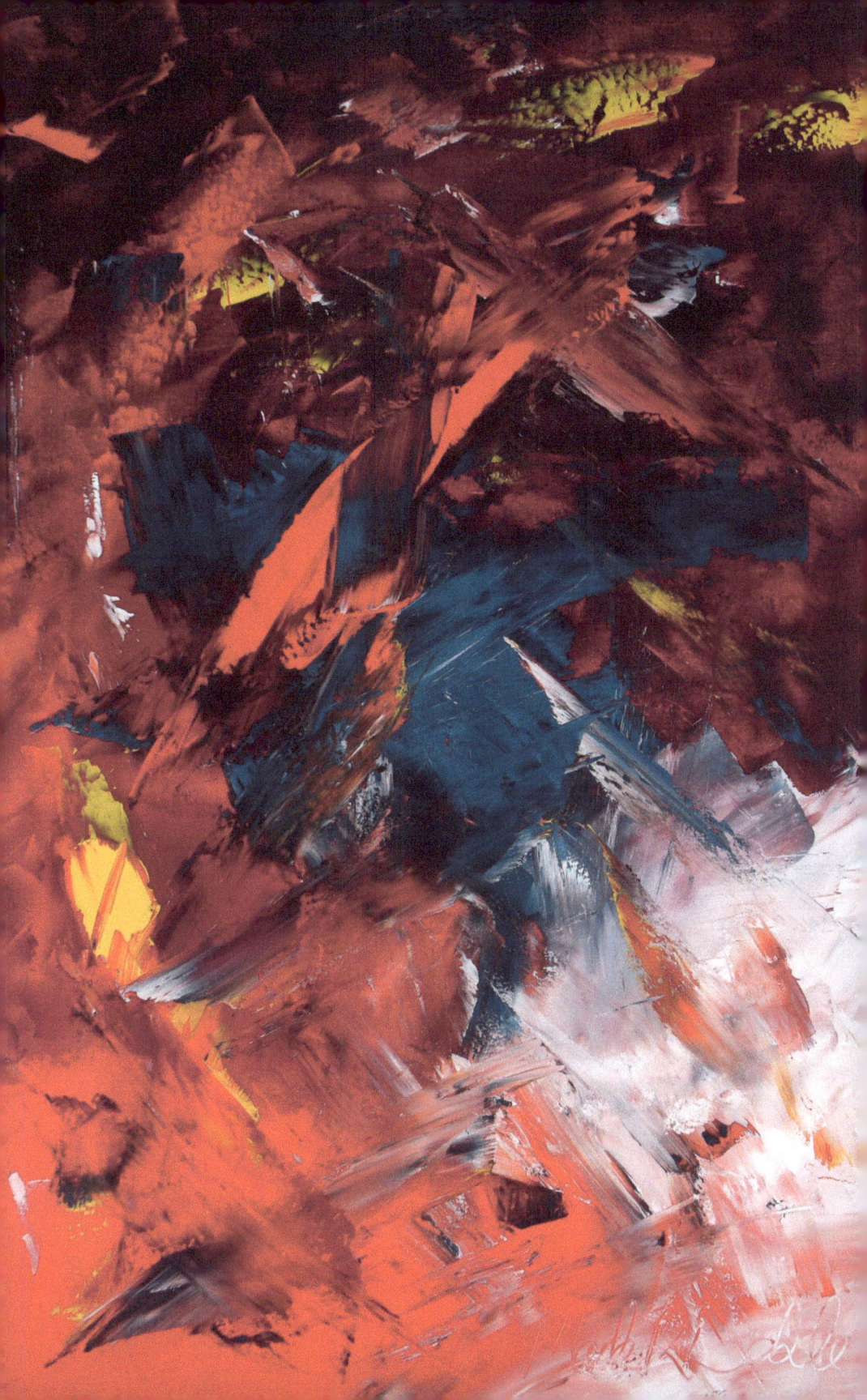

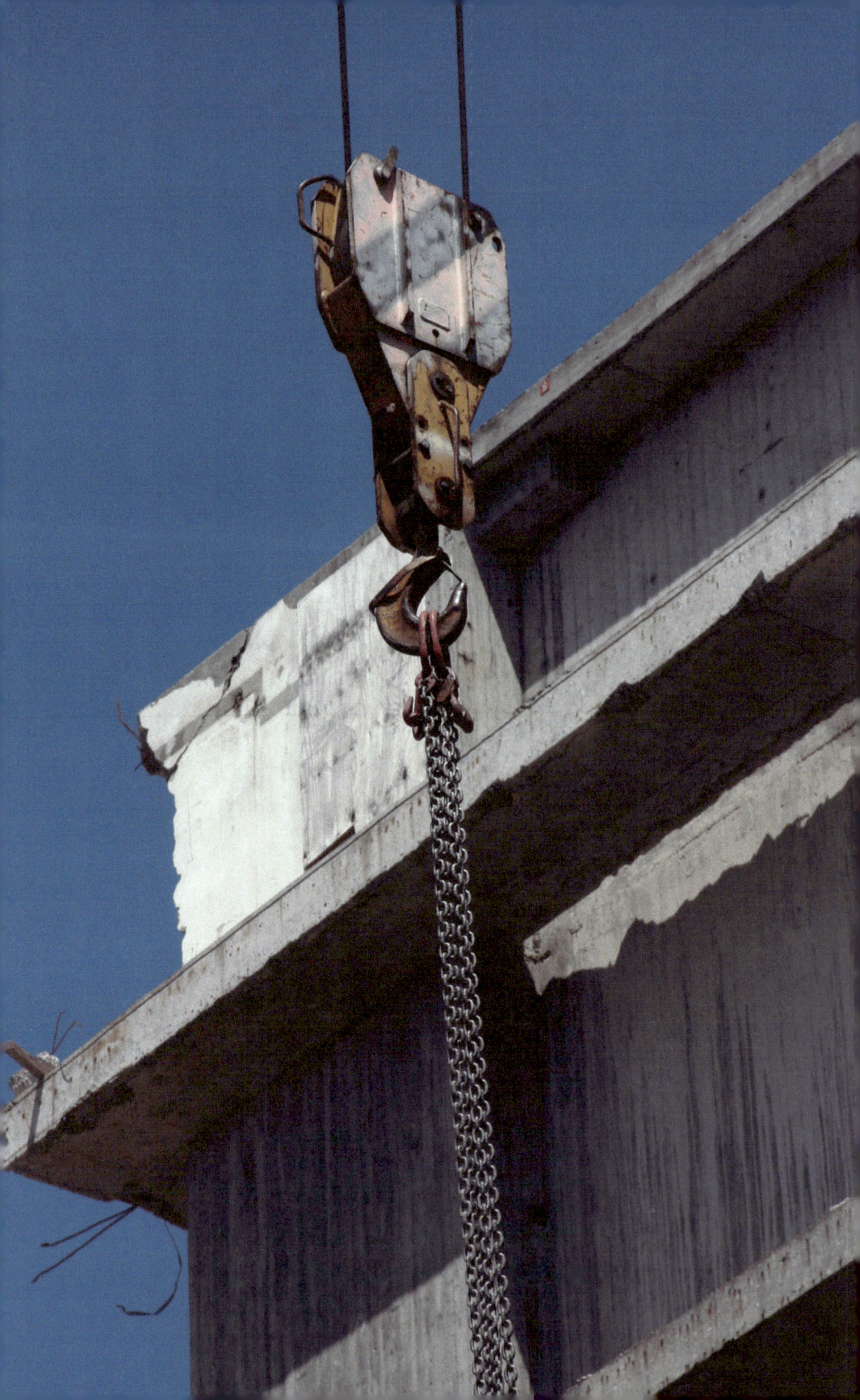

Long before Aesop became a great story teller, before Aesop met Helen and fell in love, before Alex and Athena and Alice and Kit and Lander were born and gave them joy, Aesop himself was born.

This is the story of Aesop's rather rough beginning.

When Aesop was born and was presented to his mother, she gasped and refused to hold him.

He might have been dead within hours had it not been for the love of a midwife who had compassion.

The midwife herself had been astonished at Aesop's appearance. At hundreds of deliveries she had said, "Keep pushing! Your baby's beautiful! Keep pushing!" But this time the words got stuck. "Keep pushing!" she said. "Your baby's –" and she couldn't say it. Aesop was not beautiful.

"Keep pushing!" she had said. "Your baby's almost here."

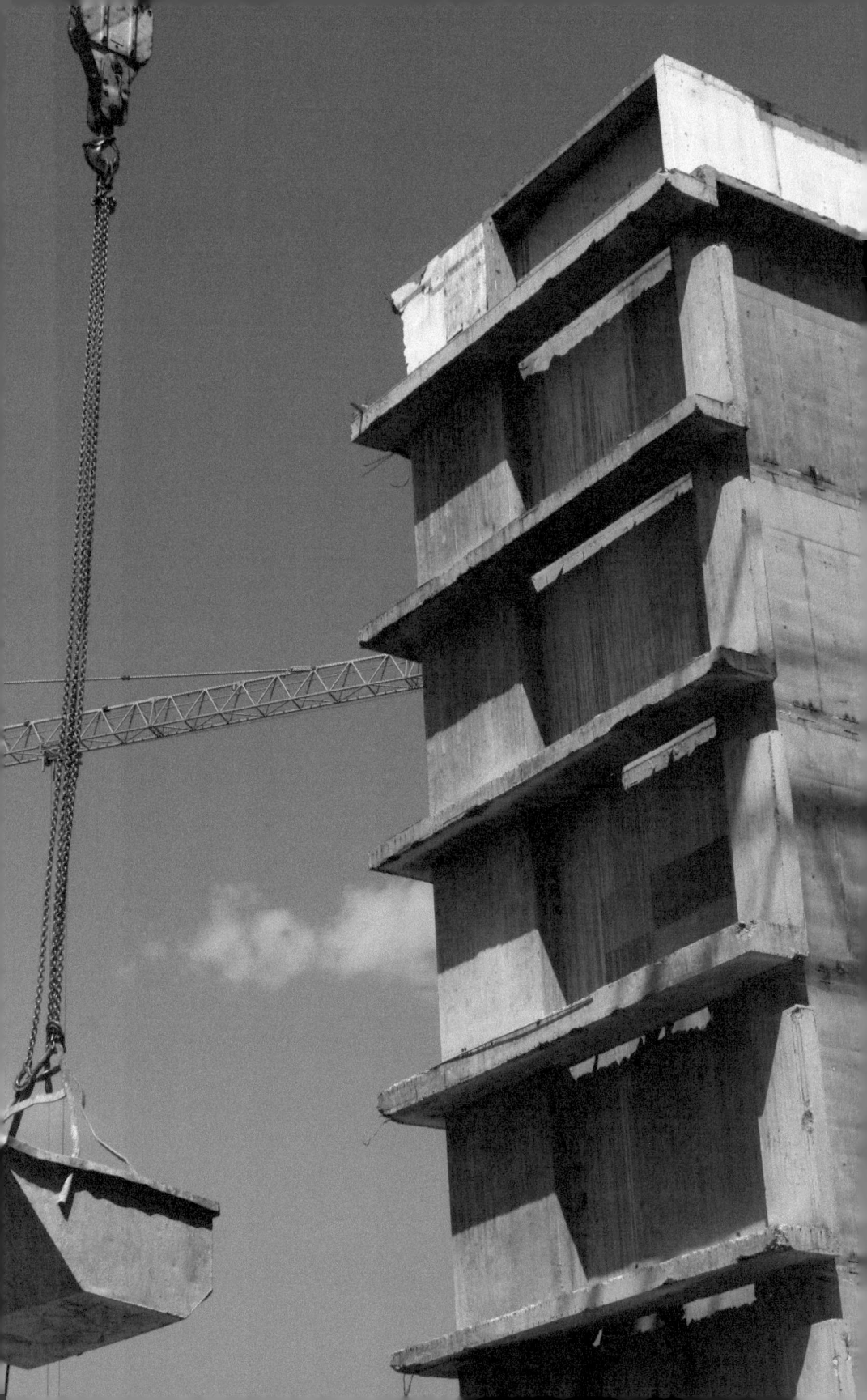

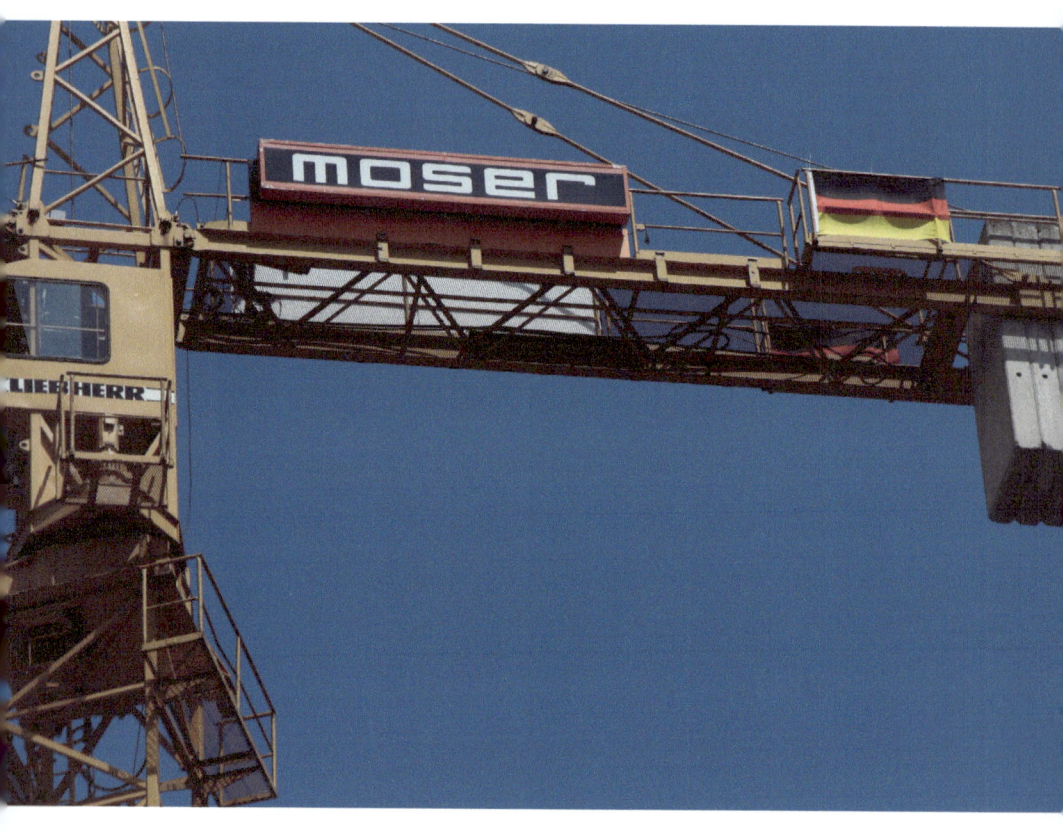

When the midwife gave Aesop to his mother, she turned away.

"No." It was all she said.

The mother's response jarred the midwife and the others standing by, but what could be done? The midwife held the baby while she tried to console the mother and get her to change her mind. But after a while, the mother's refusal and the baby's need for care caused the midwife to do something she had never done before: she adopted the baby as her own.

Octavia wasn't sure what made this baby different for her. Other mothers had refused to care for babies if they were deformed or somehow imperfect. Over the years Octavia had seen a number of unwanted babies left on the rocks above the town. But this one, for some reason, this one she rescued. Octavia was the one who named him Aesop.

Octavia's daughter agreed to nurse Aesop, but the primary care for the child fell on the midwife herself. As a result, she brought him with her to every delivery, initially in a basket with a blanket covering his face.

Octavia's care and provision for Aesop in his early years were extraordinary – especially so, given her age and the limits of her income. Many wonderful moments might be mentioned. But Octavia did one remarkable thing for Aesop that *must* be told. She made up a story that changed his life.

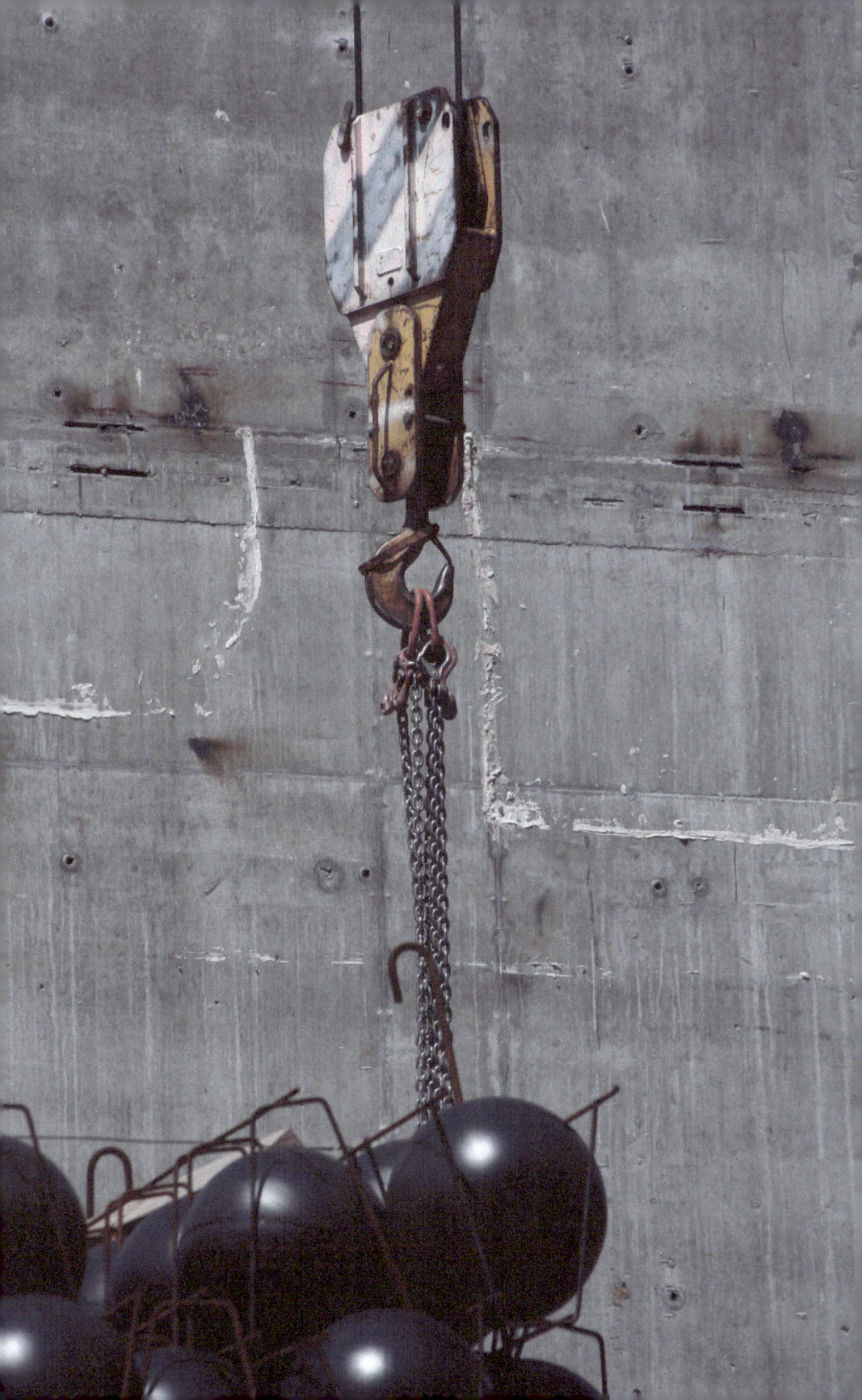

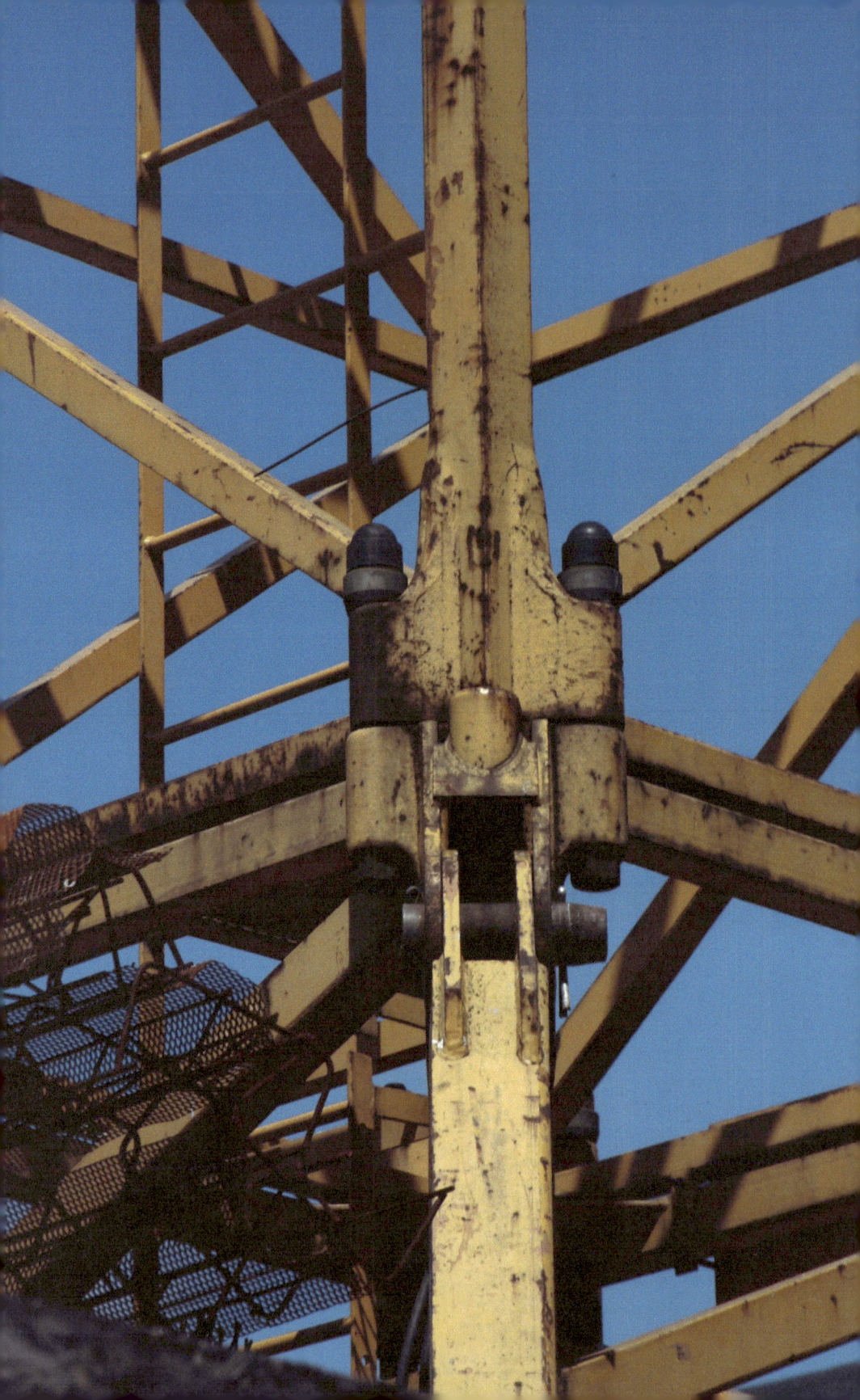

As the word about Aesop's birth and appearance spread, some of the pregnant women that Octavia assisted wondered if it were safe to have Aesop in their houses when they delivered – perhaps he would bring bad luck to their own deliveries. Octavia confronted the whispers head-on.

"Did you know," she asked a group of women soon to become mothers, "every time Aesop comes along with me, the deliveries go better than expected? They're much less painful. It's been remarkable. And it's not just the deliveries that go better. Two nights ago, Damara peeked into the basket to look at Aesop before Taren was born. The next day her husband was promoted." Exclamations of surprise filled the room, with affirmations from the few who had already heard about the promotion.

Octavia pressed her point. "I can't tell you how many mothers and fathers have been thanking me for bringing Aesop along. Everyone says having Aesop in their houses has brought them good luck. Did you know Naiyah's elderly father recovered right after Aesop's visit? And Tia had something wonderful happen, too, but it's a secret and I can't tell you what it was."

When the young women started talking about blessings that had come to their friends after Aesop visited, each could name two or three.

One thought of a counter-example: an accident that had occurred the day after Aesop had been in the house of her best friend.

Luckily Octavia was quick-witted enough to respond to the challenge. "That *was* terrible, wasn't it?" she asked, looking right into the young girl's eyes. "Can you imagine how *bad* it might have been if Aesop hadn't been there blessing the house the day before?"

With that, a clamor of voices arose asking Octavia to be sure to bring Aesop when she arrived for her midwife duties.

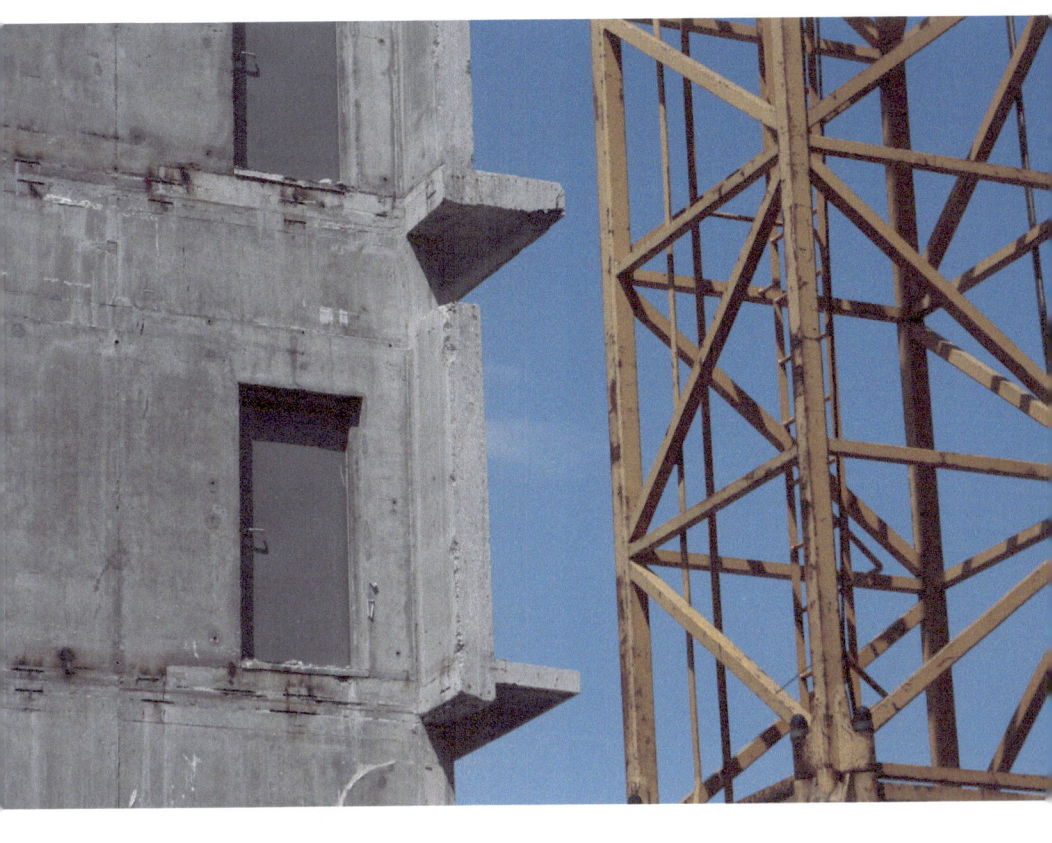

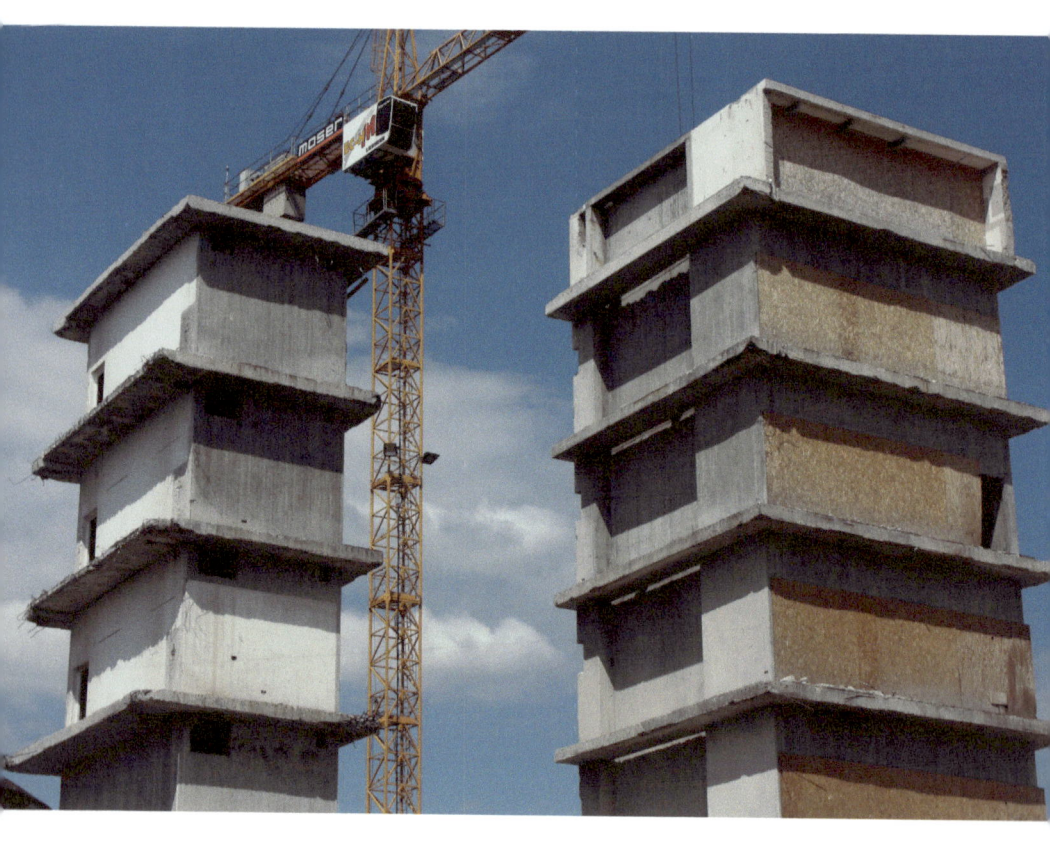

That conversation probably would have been enough to cement Aesop's acceptance in the community. But the clincher happened a few days later. Some of the young women, unable to get over their curiosity, visited Tia to ask what her good luck had been after Aesop's visit. Tia had blushed and giggled and then refused to say. As a result, each of Tia's visitors guessed something she privately thought wonderful. Perhaps Aesop's luck would help her own fantasies come true. The young women insisted on Octavia as their midwife – but only if she brought Aesop.

Octavia was probably the best midwife in the county and she had been popular before. But once people heard that having Aesop present at the delivery brought a blessing to the house, Octavia found herself in constant demand. She brought Aesop everywhere she went, and the custom developed that Aesop should be observed (or even touched or held) before the birth of a child. By the time Aesop was a toddler, he was known to most of the families in the county, both rich and poor.

Aesop's appearance did not improve as he grew, but people overlooked it since he brought good luck. Eventually the locals were so used to how he looked that they gave it little thought.

By the time he was ten, Aesop knew the names, addresses and occupations of more people in the city than anyone else. He had been in all their houses. For a boy with his appearance, he could hardly have been luckier, at least among adults.

Among his own peers, it was a different story. A few of his acquaintances admired his pluck. In addition, a few behaved politely towards him because their parents were desperate for better times and insisted that Aesop occasionally come over and be treated well. But Aesop had no real friends his age, and his afternoons were miserable because of the bullies.

Three in particular sought him out: Javan, Tad and Damian. The boys hated everything Aesop. Because Aesop loved animals and often went on long walks to observe them, they began hating and torturing animals, too.

One day, when Aesop was ten, he was captured by the three bullies. Javan had just turned twelve; Tad and Damian were each eleven. They had brought a frog and were going to torture it in Aesop's presence before beating him up.

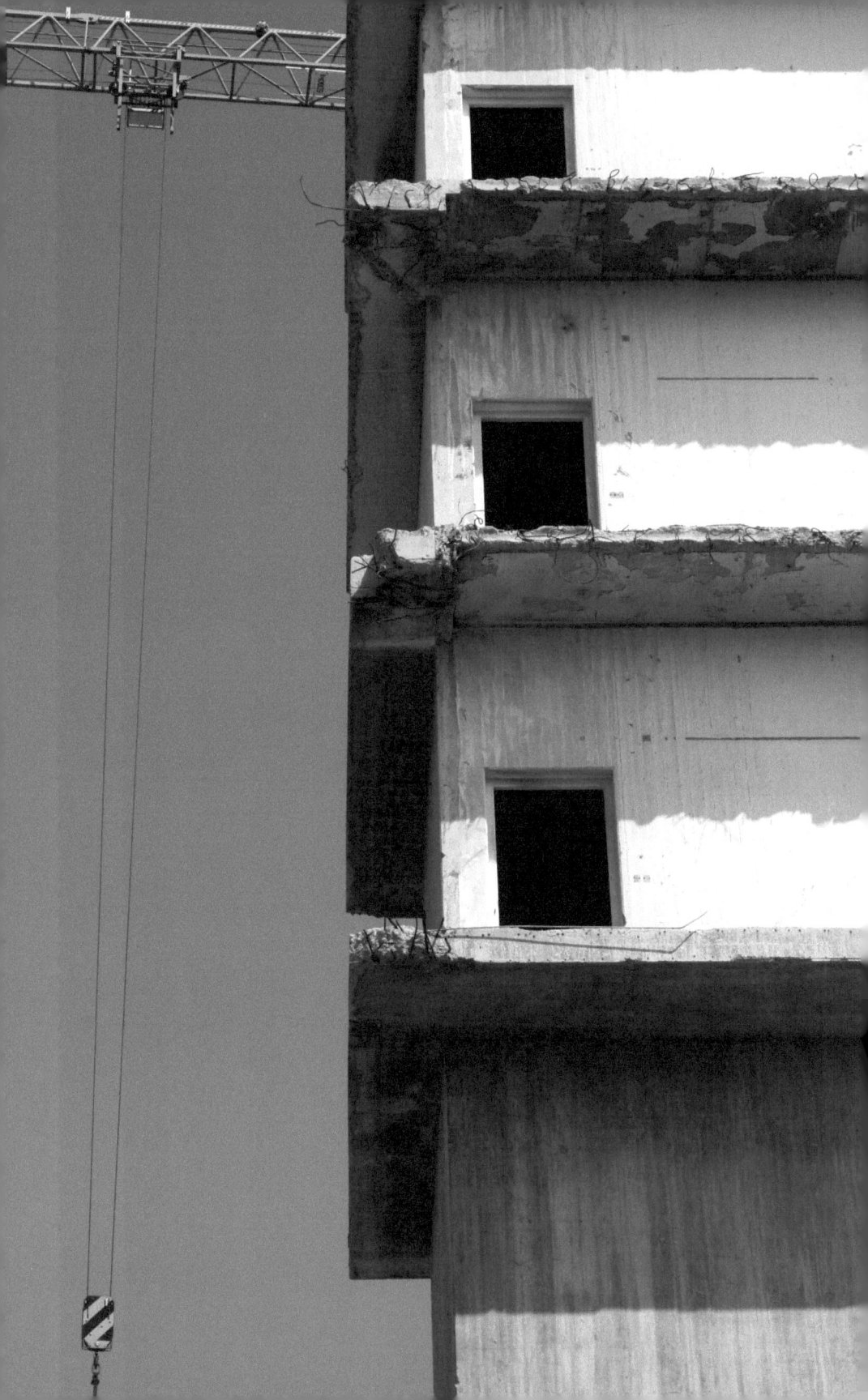

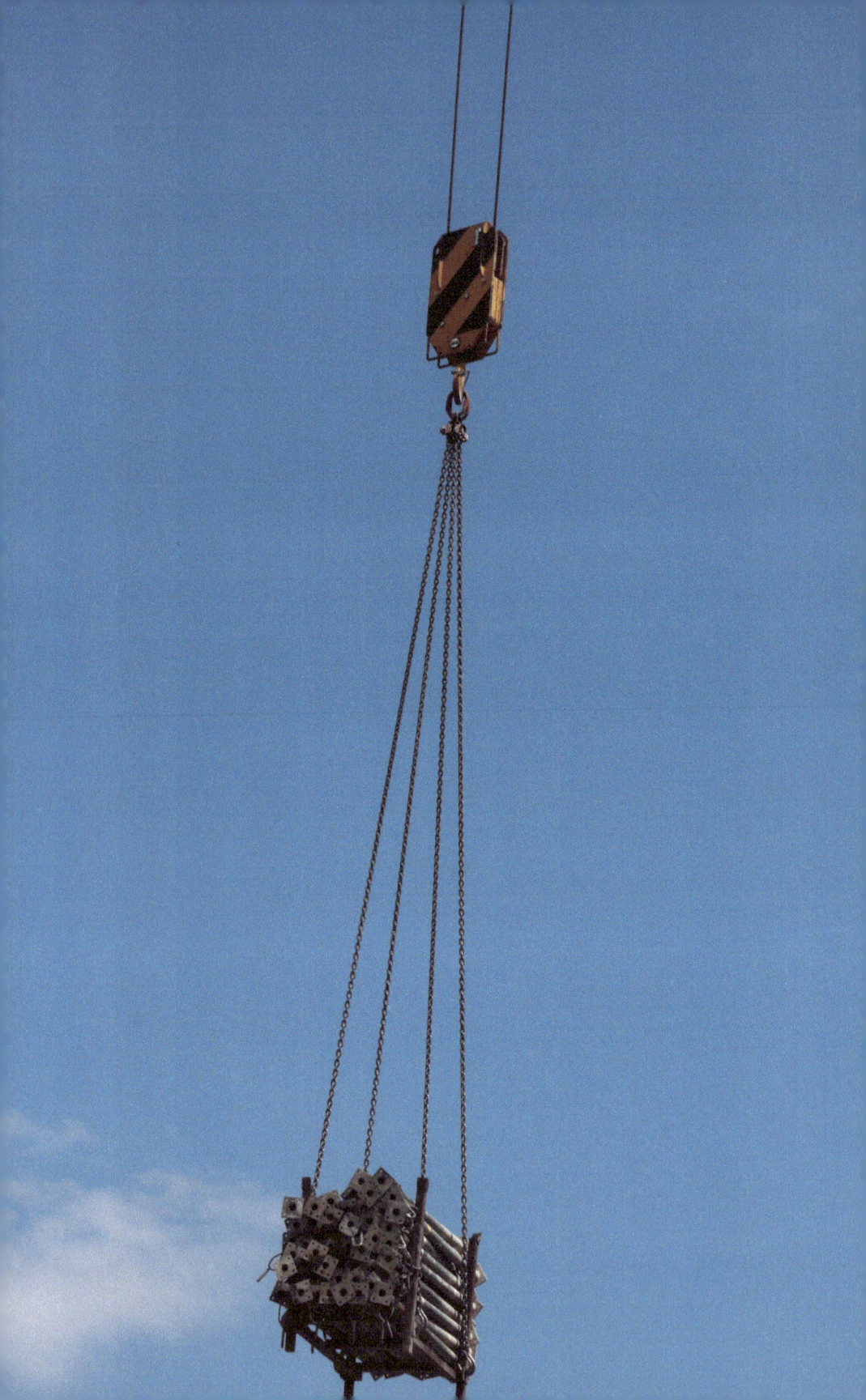

Aesop might have withstood another beating on his own without comment. But because they were going to harm the frog, he protested. "Stop!" he said.

Javan laughed. "Hey! He speaks! We should get more frogs and see what other words he knows."

"Stop!" Aesop said again, unsure what to say next, unsure what would make a difference to these three. "That frog will bring you luck."

It was all he could come up with on short notice – his own story that had saved him so much grief and disappointment. But Javan and his friends weren't buying it.

"Hah!" Javan said. "My dad says *you* bring good luck. 'Why can't you be like Aesop,' " he mimicked. " 'I'd rather have *him* for a son than you.' That's what my dad said last night before he belted me. My dad wants me to be an ugly pug like you. So today I'm going to make you wish you kept some of your luck for yourself. You like animals, so you get to watch what we do to this frog. Then we're going to take care of you."

Aesop knew the frog's life depended on what he said next.

"If you let the frog go," he said, "I will tell you what kind of luck he can bring you – and what you can do to get it."

Javan broke one of the frog's legs in response, glaring at Aesop.

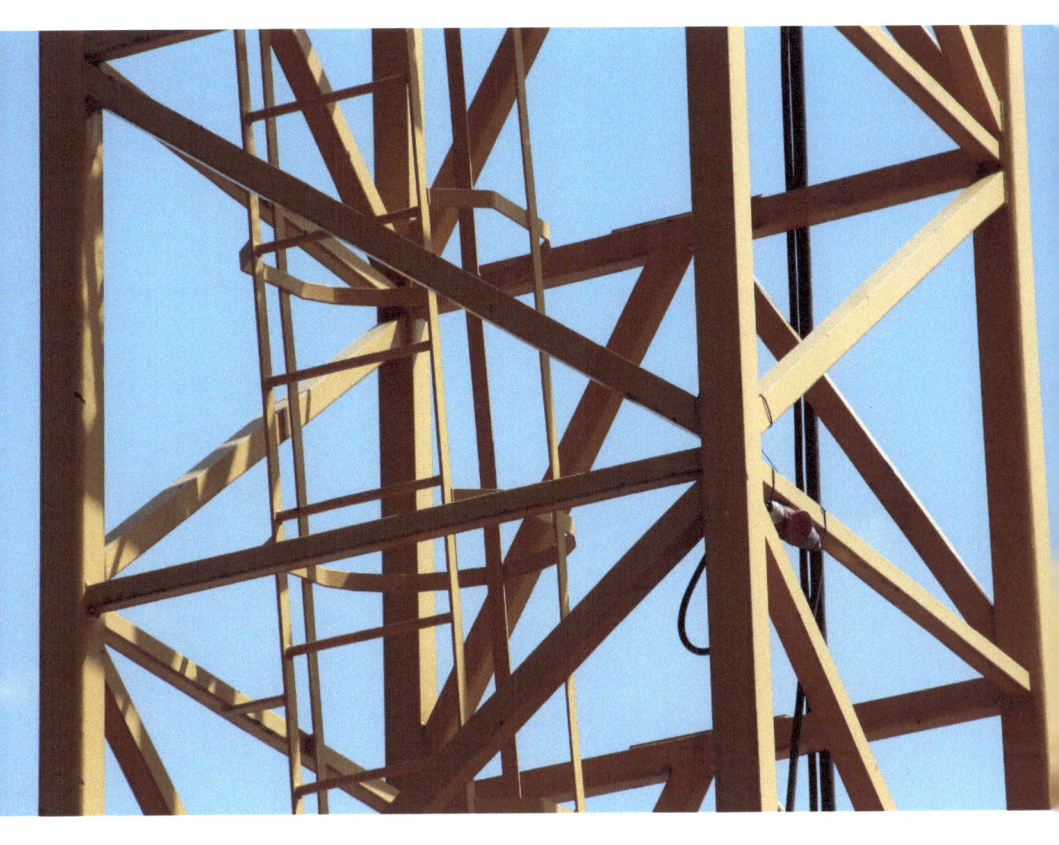

23

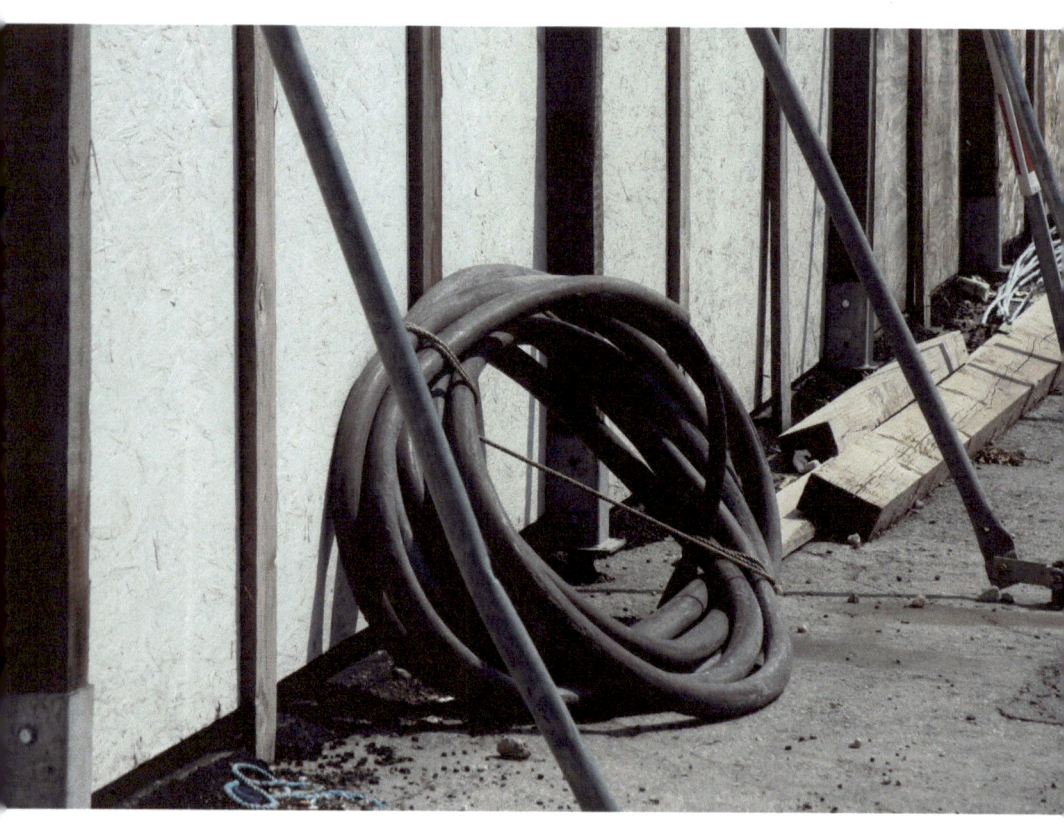

"Wait!" shouted Tad. "Wait! Let Aesop tell us."

Javan slowly turned to his friend. "What?" he asked. "Are you *siding* with Aesop? We can fix you, too, you know."

Tad opened and shut his mouth. He was determined not to cry. But Tad was fighting a fear greater than his fear of Javan. Earlier in the day Tad had passed The Broken Wheel and seen his father inside. When his father started the morning at Pancho's pub, the nights at his house were dreadful. Tad's terror of what he would face at home that night overwhelmed his fear of being turned on by his friends. He snapped.

"I don't care about Aesop *or* your stupid frog," he said. "But stop being a fool. You should listen to him first. If you don't like what he says, *then* you can beat him up." He glared at Javan.

Javan blinked. He was used to calling the shots, and he was *not* used to being called a fool. But once the hot flash of anger subsided, he realized he had no intention of turning on Tad and breaking up his gang. It was all he had.

"Okay," he said gruffly, at least as gruffly as a twelve-year-old can. "Okay." He put the frog down. "Aesop – this had better be good."

Now it was Aesop's turn to be fearful. He had no story in mind. Watching the frog struggle to move away from the scene with a broken leg filled him with such compassion and anxiety that he could think of nothing but the frog's misery.

"I can't," Aesop said at last.

Javan took a step towards him.

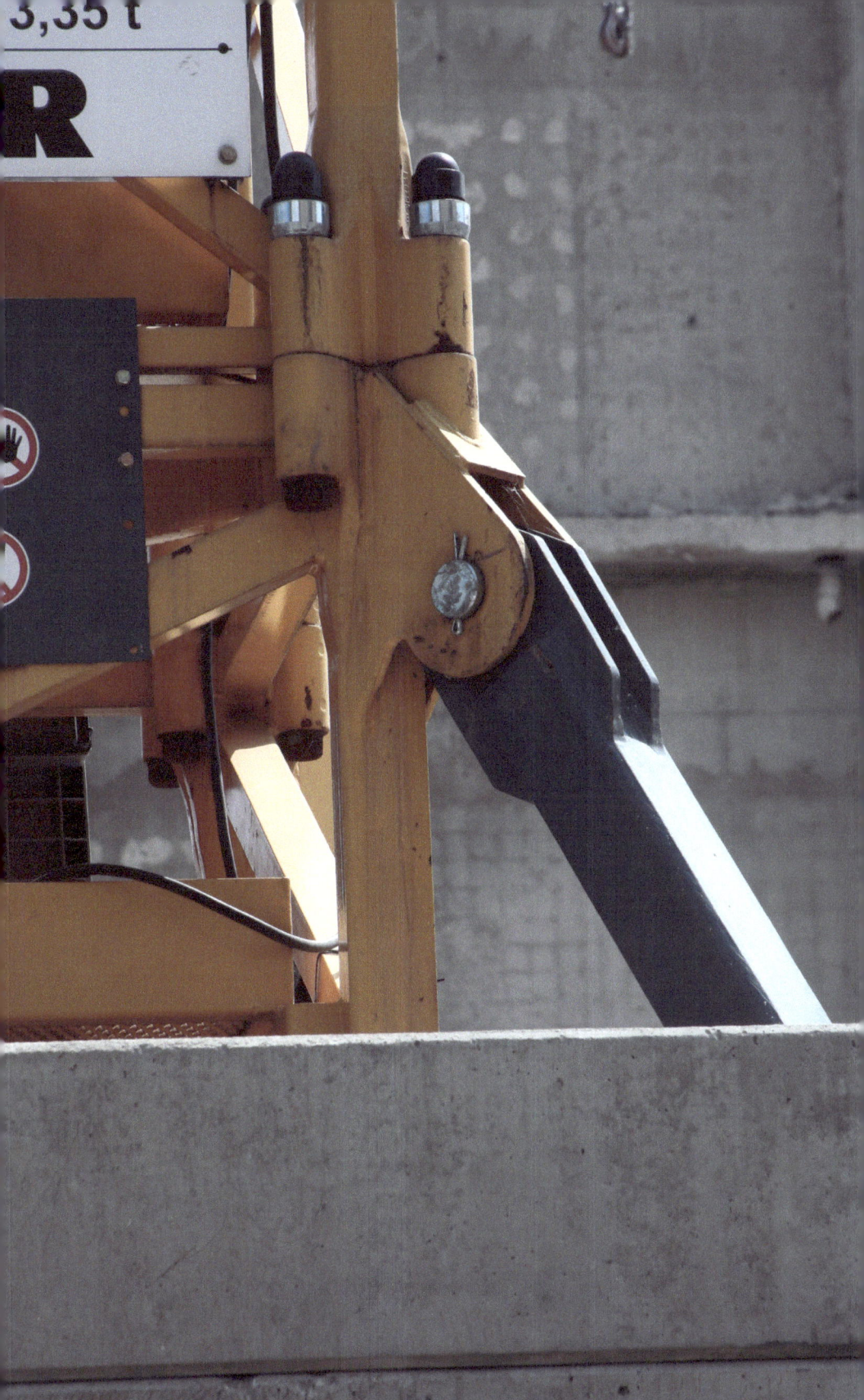

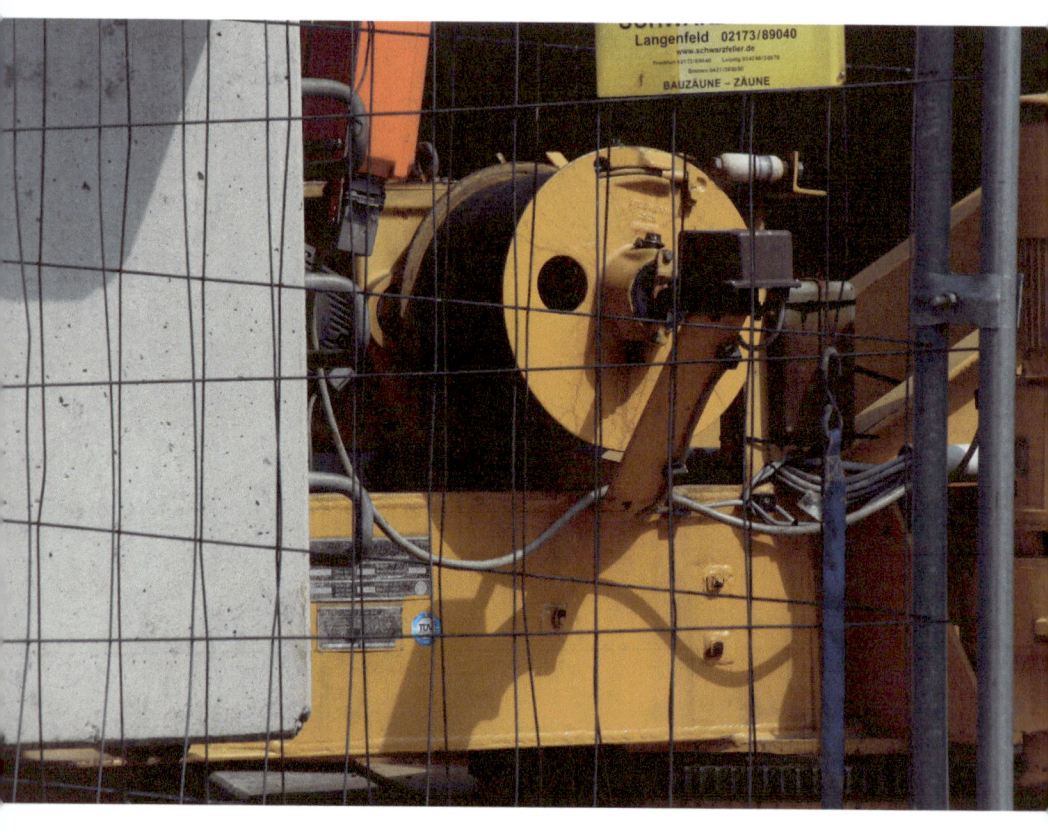

"I can't," Aesop repeated. "I mean, look at him," pointing to the frog. "He can't even hop. How can he give good luck today?"

Aesop resigned himself to being beat up again. But he said the only thing that came to him. "Meet me here tomorrow. I'll tell you tomorrow."

On any other day, this comment would never have worked with Javan. But today Tad was desperate. He did not want to miss out on the chance of a change at home – *any* kind of change – and he did *not* want to wait until the next day. To the surprise of his friends and of Aesop, Tad scooped up the frog and ran for home. Tad knew he was risking everything with his friends. He didn't care. He cradled the frog close to his chest as he ran.

Tad's house was deserted when he arrived; he put the frog in a dark corner at the back and boxed him in with a plank. Since the frog could not hop, it was enough to keep him a prisoner.

"Listen you," Tad said. "If you don't help, we could both be dead in the morning. And even if we survive tonight, tomorrow Javan will probably make us *wish* we'd died. So you better have some good luck left."

Then he went outside to find something to feed his new pet.

When night arrived, Hektor, Tad's father, had not returned. Tad curled up by his frog and fell asleep.

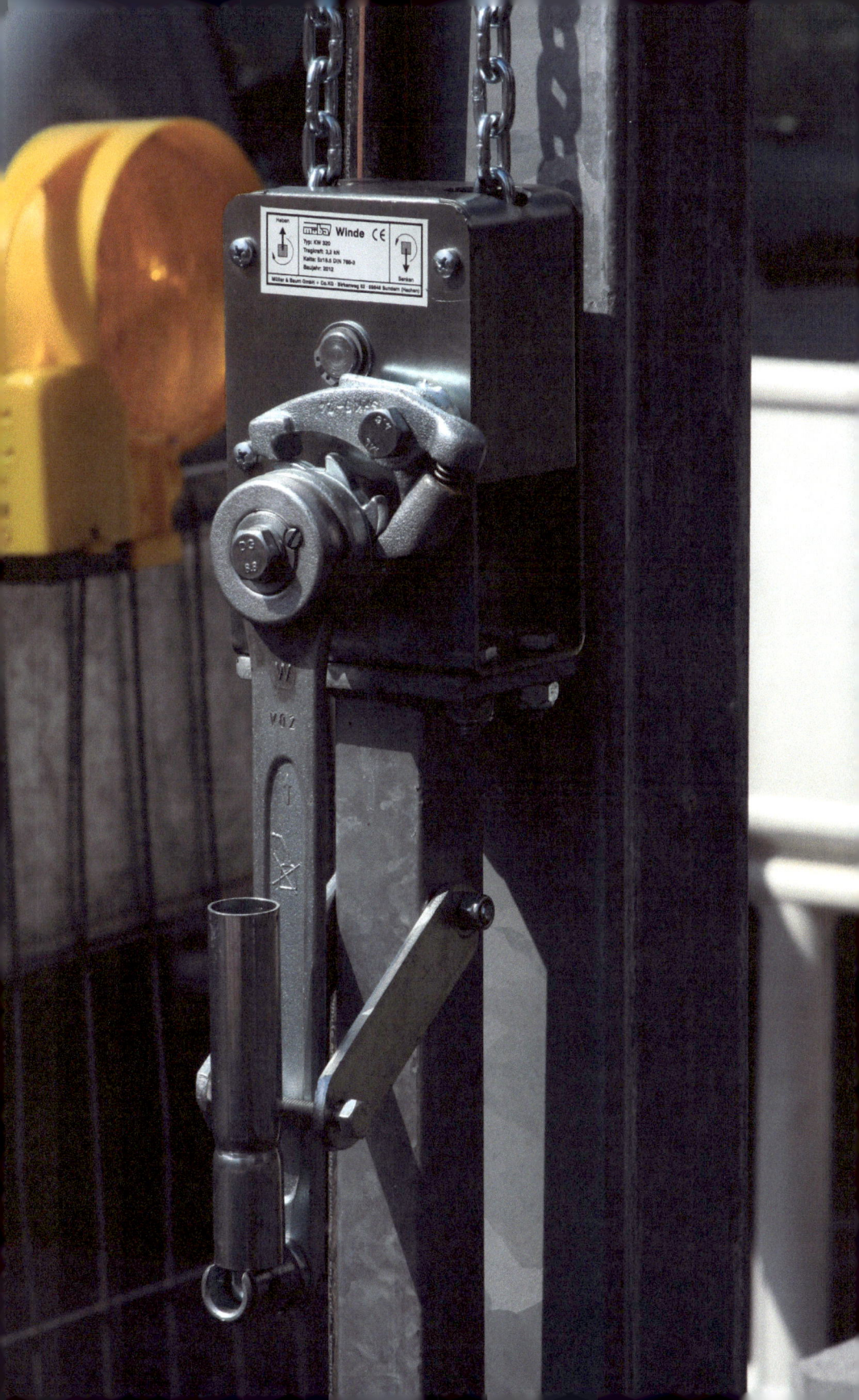

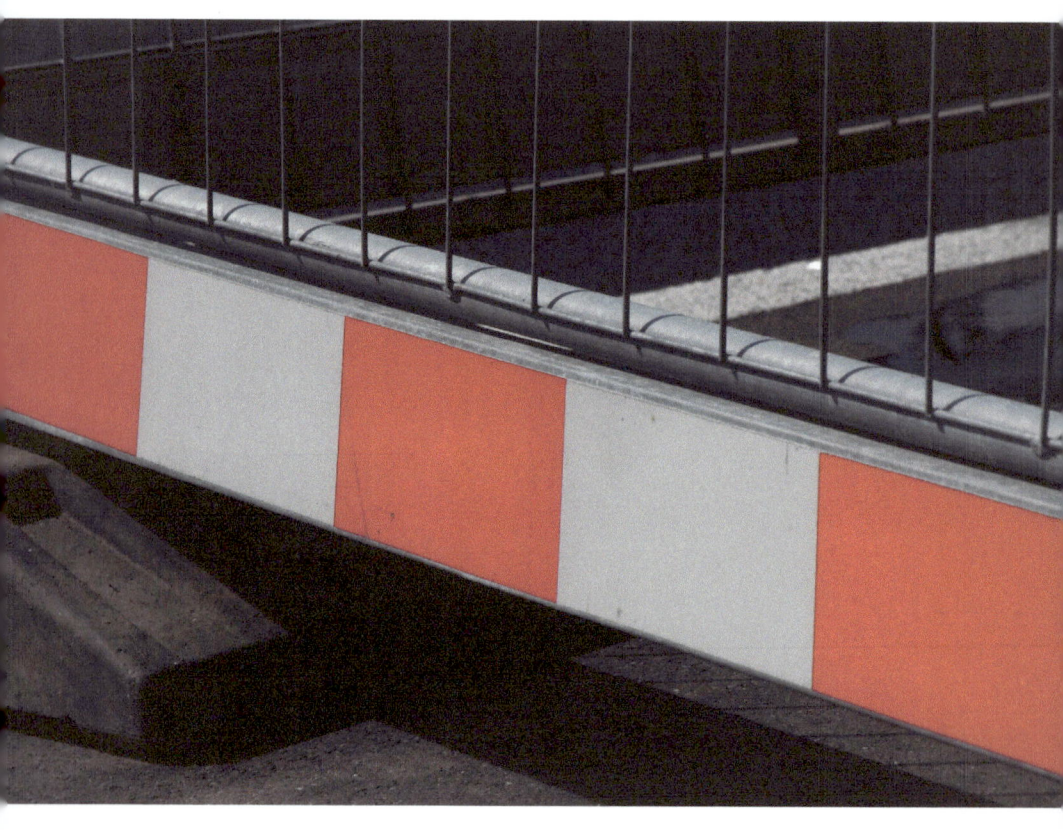

Quite a bit later, Tad woke when he heard his father trip on entering the house. He heard his dad check Tad's empty bed and curse.

"Where's that useless boy?" Hektor snarled. Then he fell.

Tad lay beside the frog the rest of the night, shivering.

In the morning Tad was surprised to have survived without a scar. He found his dad passed out near Tad's bed. But his hope disappeared when he checked on his pet. The frog was dead.

In a panic, Tad picked up the frog, edged past his snoring father, and fled the house. He hurled the frog into the meadow. He had survived the night, but *now* what would he do?

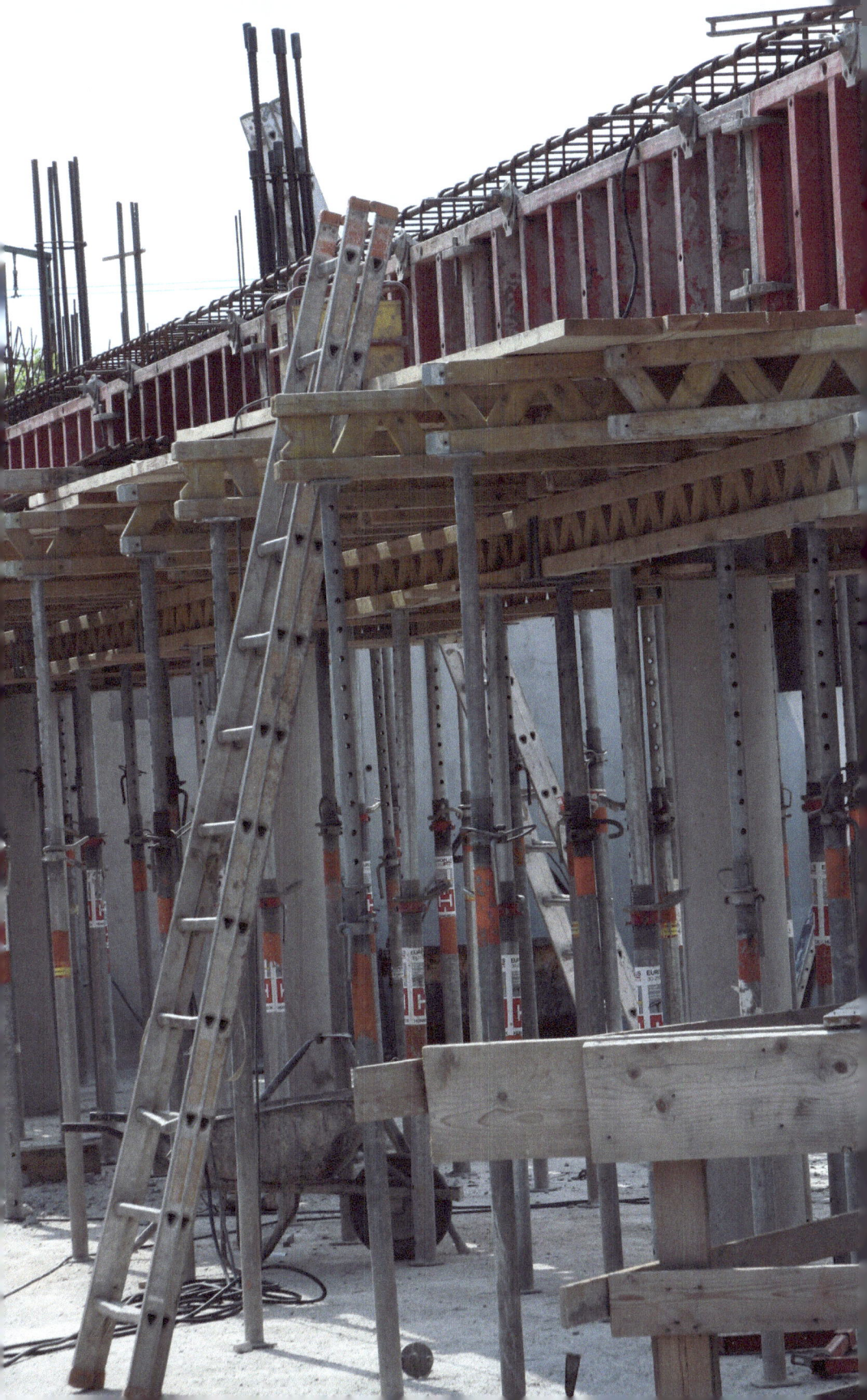

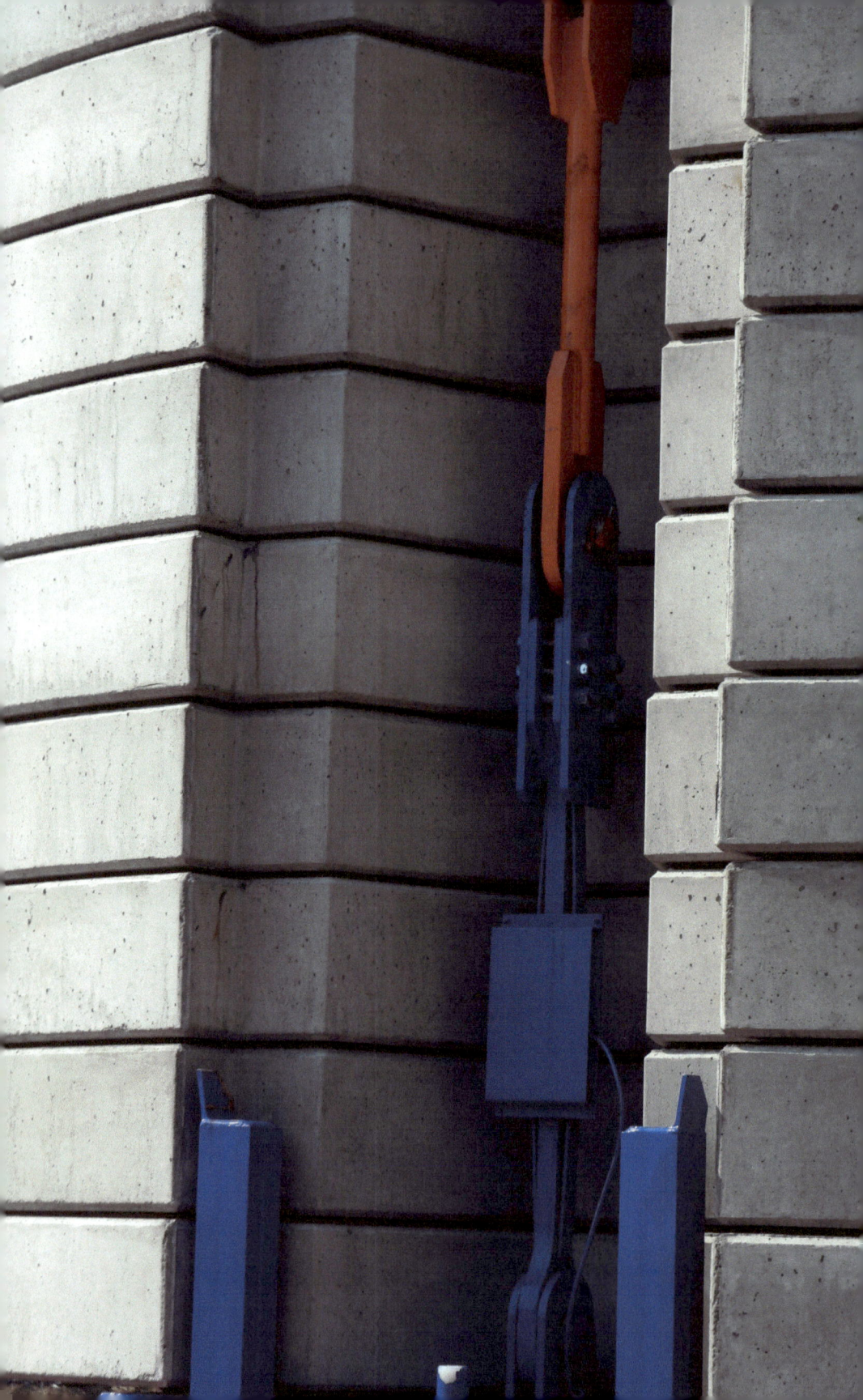

Tad's friends didn't see him at school that day. He met them on their way home. Tad had a frog in each hand. "If either of you touch these frogs, I'll kill you," he said, defiant and close to tears. "Now get Aesop."

Javan and Damian glanced at each other. Tad did not take the lead very often.

But Aesop, in fact, was already heading their way. It was his only route home, and he knew he could not escape these three forever. Better to face them head-on and see if he could talk his way out.

Before Aesop got close, he saw Tad blocking the path, holding two squirming frogs. He could tell by their movement that these frogs were new.

"Where's the other frog?" Aesop asked as he approached.

"He died," said Tad. "These are the biggest I could find to replace him. And I'll kill them myself while you watch if you don't tell me how to get good luck." The savagery in his voice caught them all off guard.

Even after a day to prepare, Aesop still had nothing to say. All he had been able to think of was his own story. But now that he saw the two frogs, he thought he could rescue at least one of them.

"This frog's no good," he said, pointing to the one on the left. "See that spot? It means he's already given his luck away. You may as well let that one go."

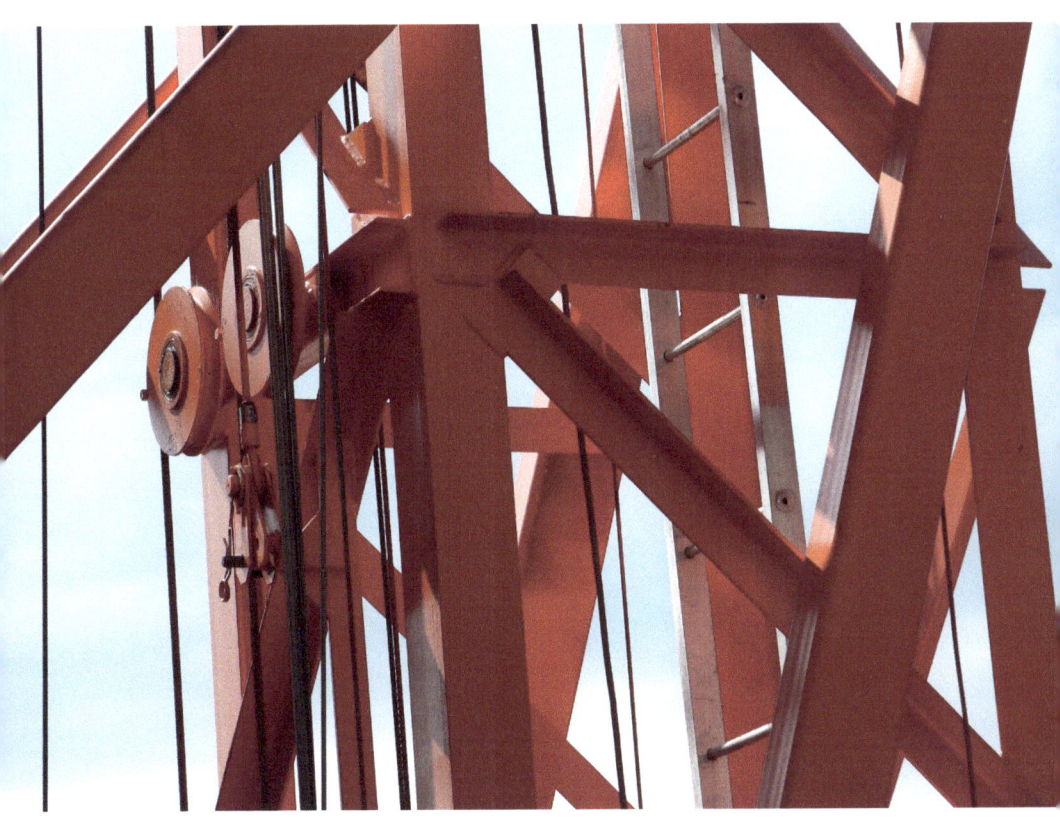

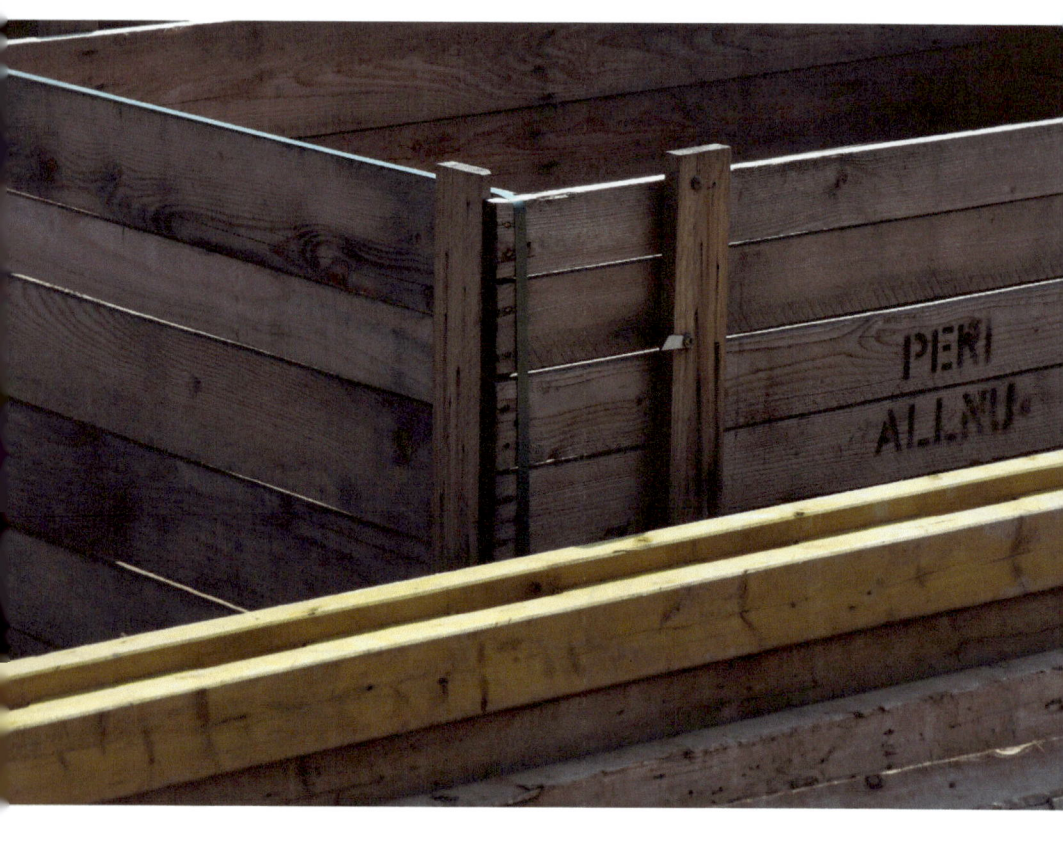

Aesop had spent enough time observing wild creatures that he caught a glimpse of the panic in Tad's eyes when he said this and adjusted his plan.

"You can let that frog go," Aesop said, "because the other one is good enough, all by himself. He's all you need."

Aesop saw Tad relax, and suddenly he knew, not in words as much as with his whole being, the terror Tad was facing and hiding, enough fear to cause him to be willing to stand up to Javan. Aesop was surprised to find himself filled with compassion. He, too, knew such fear, though for different reasons.

But Aesop still didn't know what to say. He just started talking.

"Every tadpole," Aesop said, "gets a bit of luck to give away when it's grown. Frogs can't keep the luck for themselves, but they *can* choose who to give it to. Usually frogs give their luck to people who don't bother them. I can see by looking at this one that it chose to give its luck to you. You can let it go."

Aesop could see by Tad's eyes that he was torn, not yet convinced, unwilling to let go of the one thing that had given him hope and – maybe – the one thing that had helped him survive the night.

"You don't have to hold frogs to get their luck," Aesop said, trying to reinforce the point. "All you need to do is see them from a distance. That's when they give their luck away: when they see you from a distance. And a little luck changes everything."

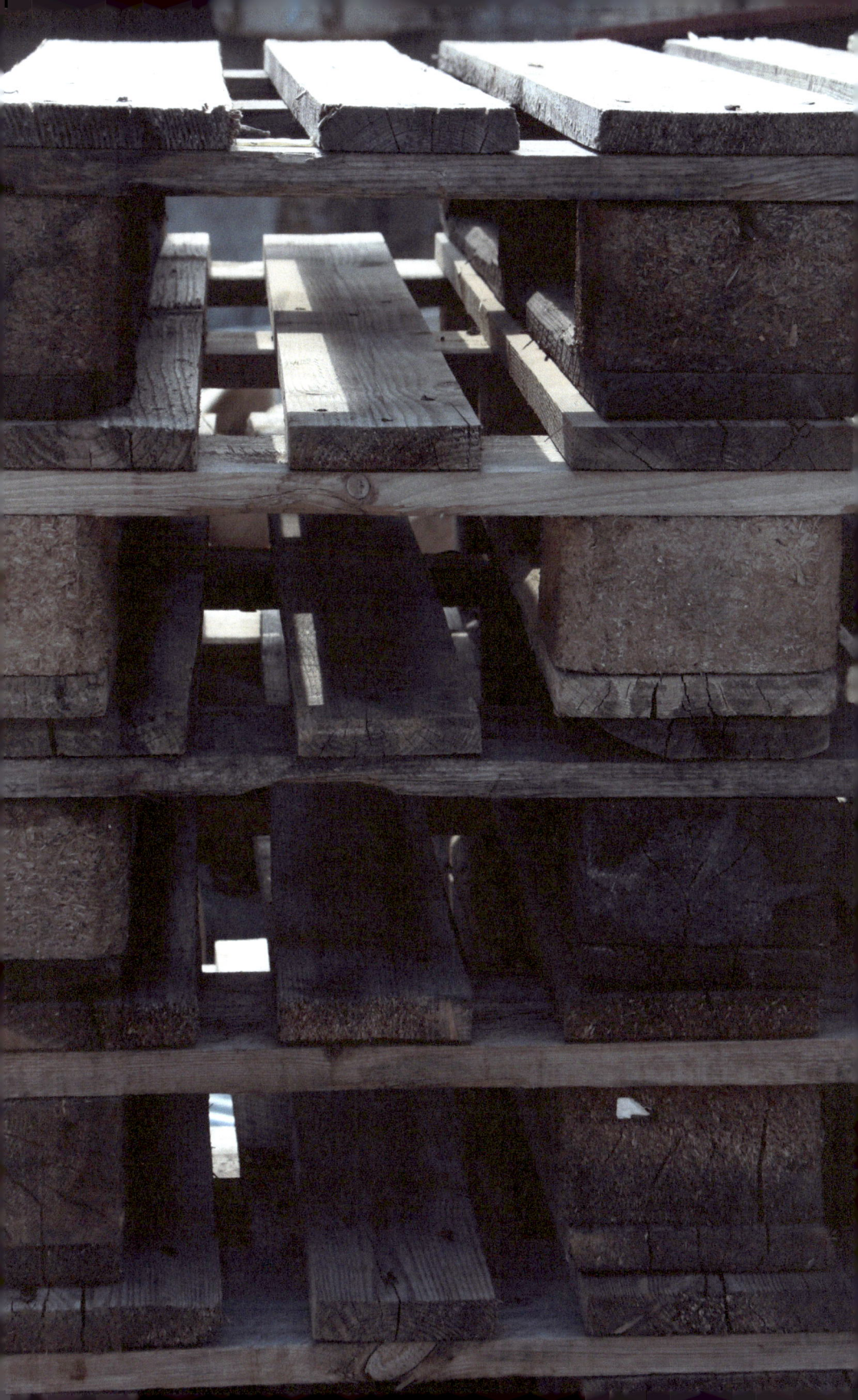

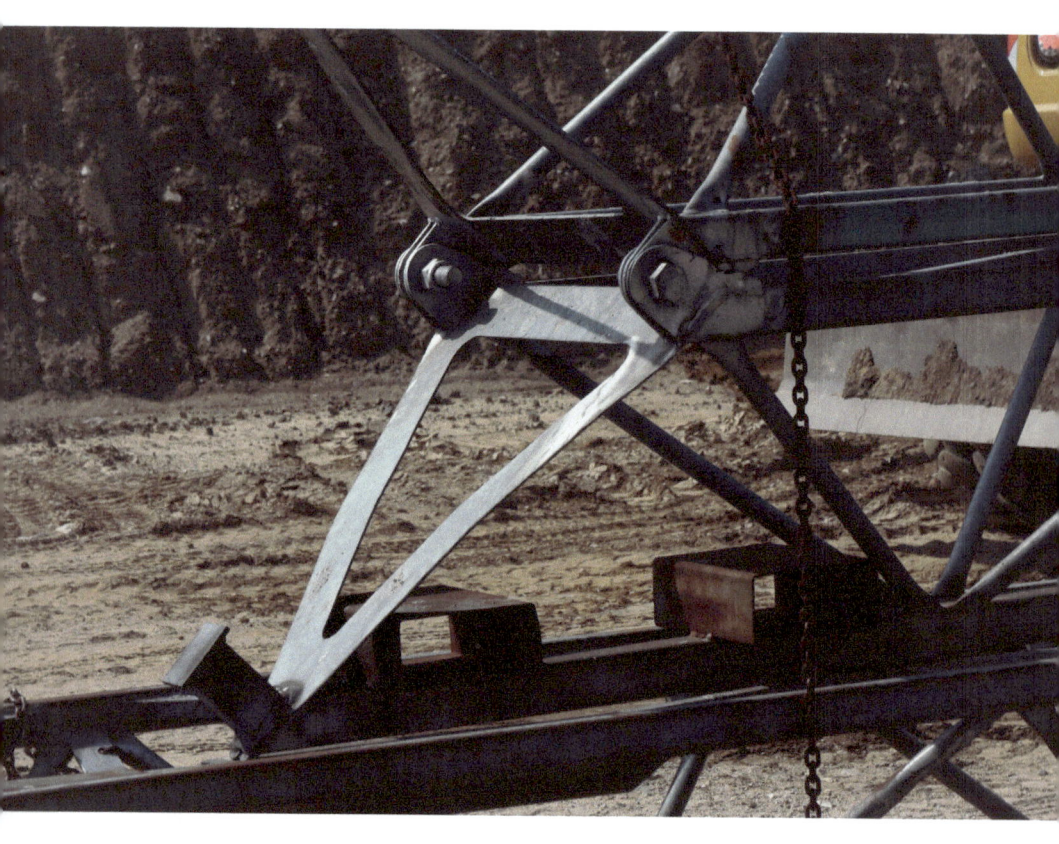

Tad thrust out his jaw and tried to look defiant. His companions could see he was still close to tears. He set the frog down. Then he wandered away.

"Where are you going?" Javan hollered.

"Home," Tad said. But he was heading the direction of the swamp.

After a pause, Aesop took a chance and started walking down the path towards his own home. Javan let him pass.

Aesop walked home in wonder. He hadn't gotten beat up. All he'd done was tell a story about a frog, and he hadn't gotten beat up.

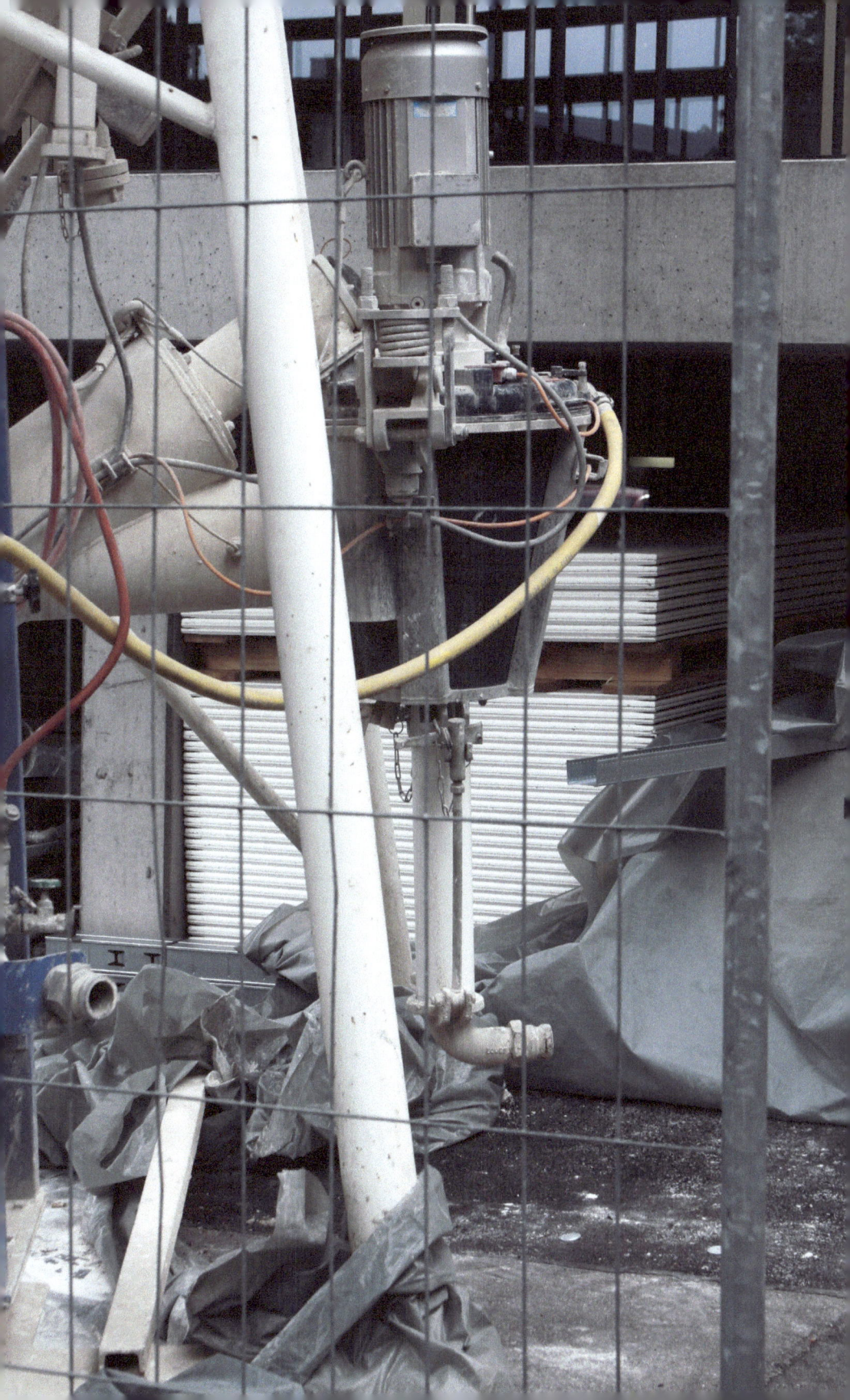

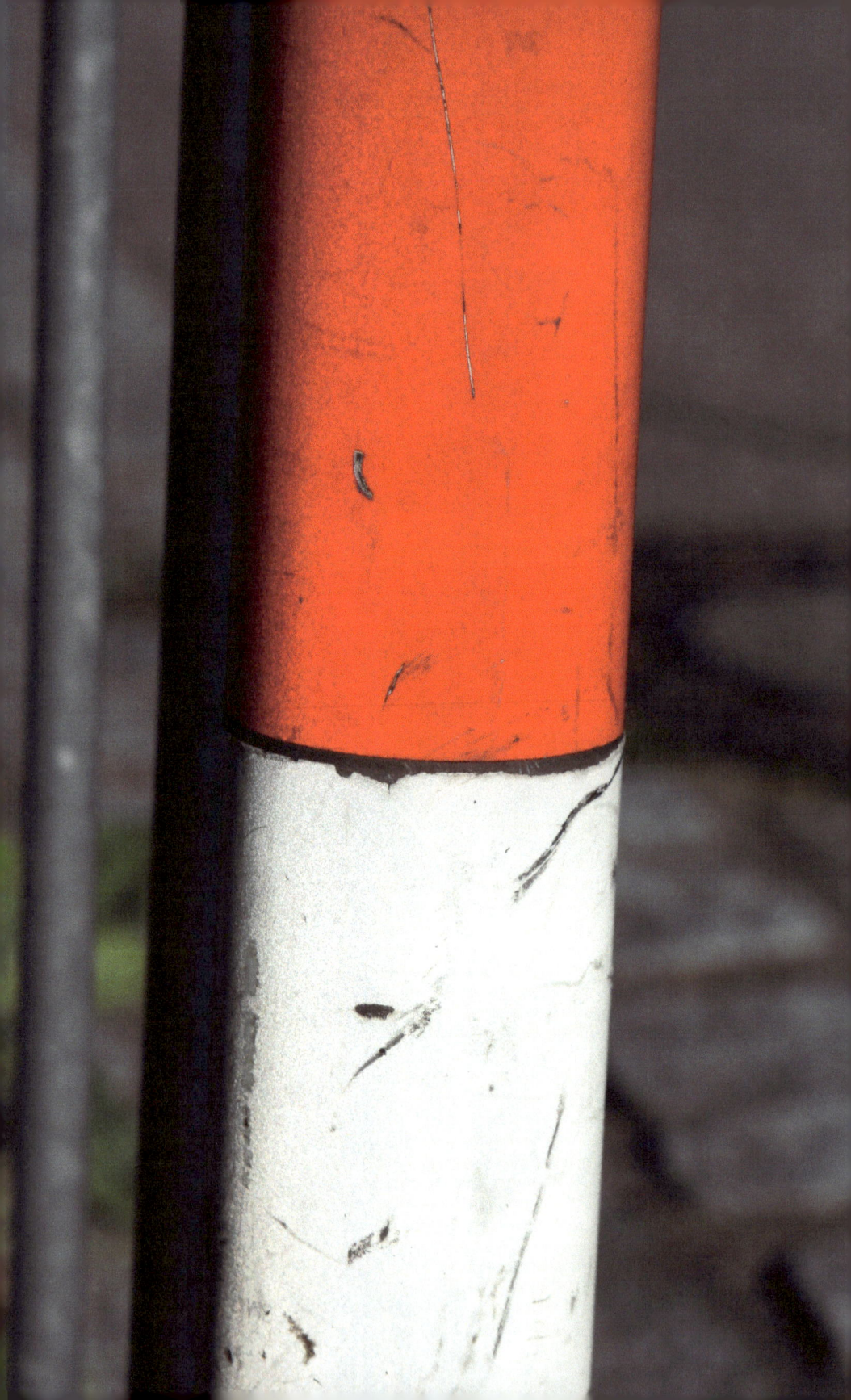

That was the day that Aesop was really born, at least the Aesop that you know.

Up to that time, Aesop had always watched animals, partly out of curiosity and partly because he had no close friends to hang out with. But now as he walked home he was wondering what animal he could talk about tomorrow. Maybe tomorrow he wouldn't get beat up, either.

A little luck changes everything, Aesop thought. A little luck can change your life.

~~

Reflection questions

Is Aesop lucky? Why or why not?

When the young women started considering ways their friends had been blessed after Octavia visited with Aesop, they could think of many examples. What do you think of the idea that if you look for luck you'll find some?

If it were true that you find what you look for, what would *you* want to look for?

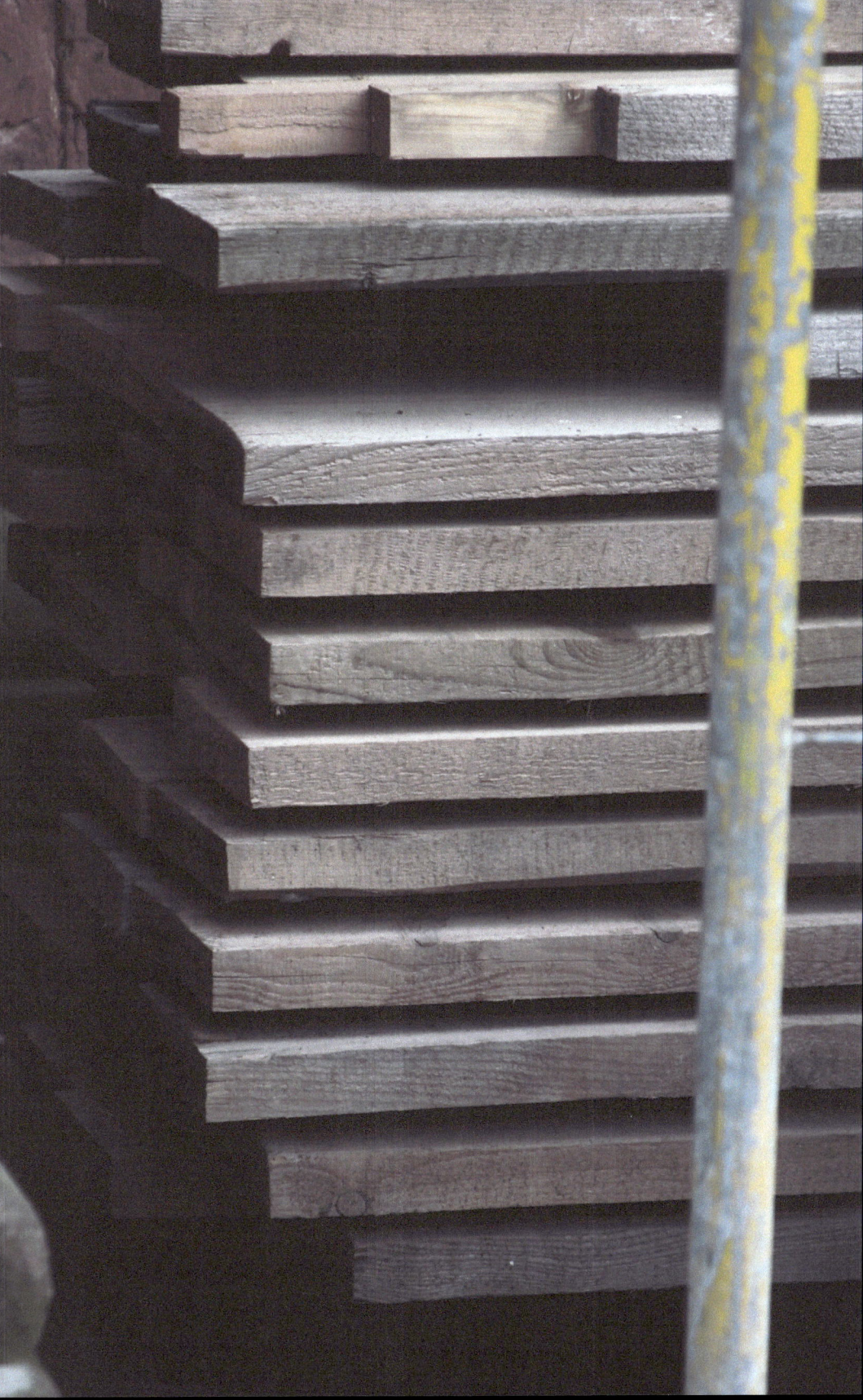

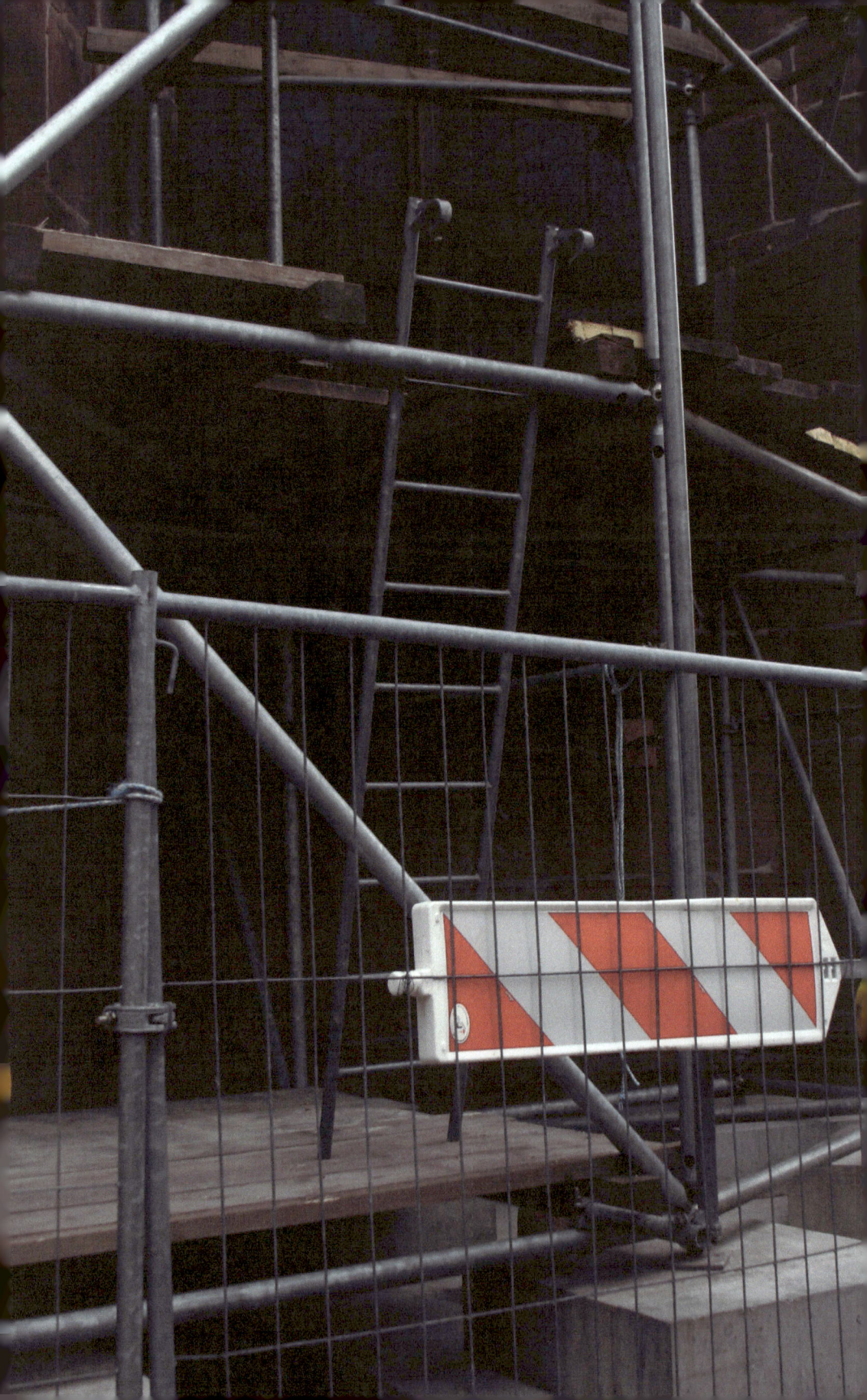

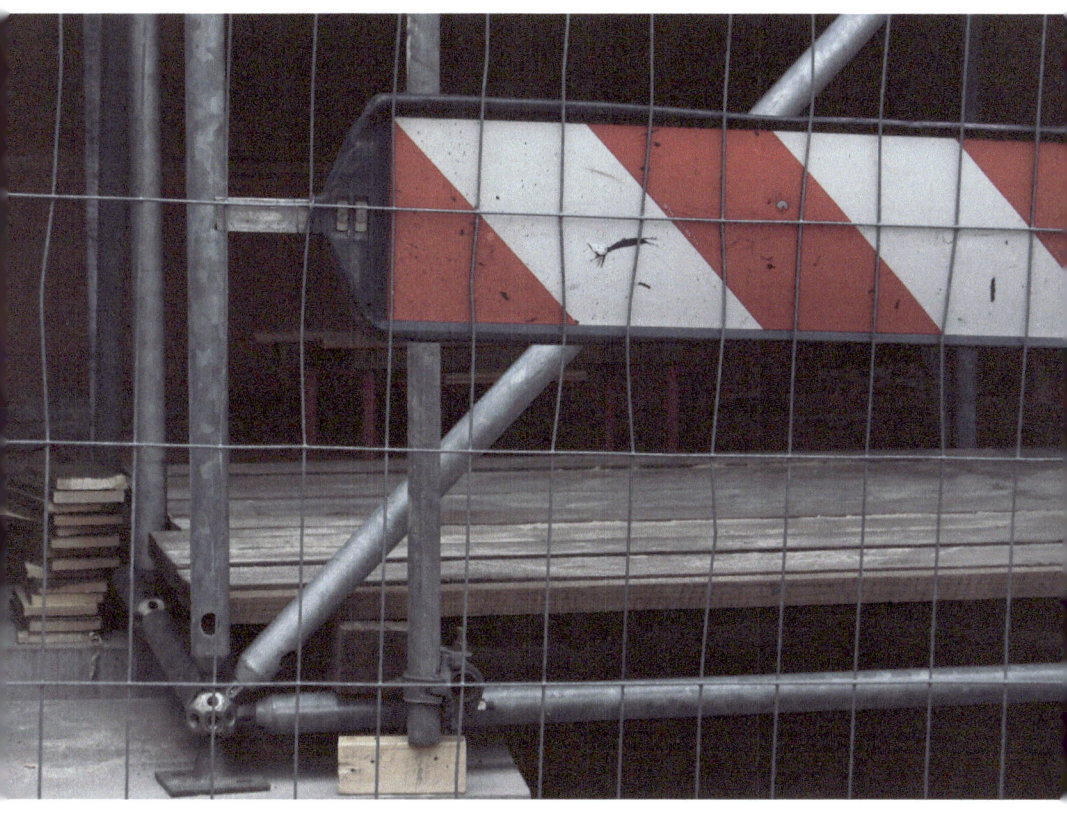

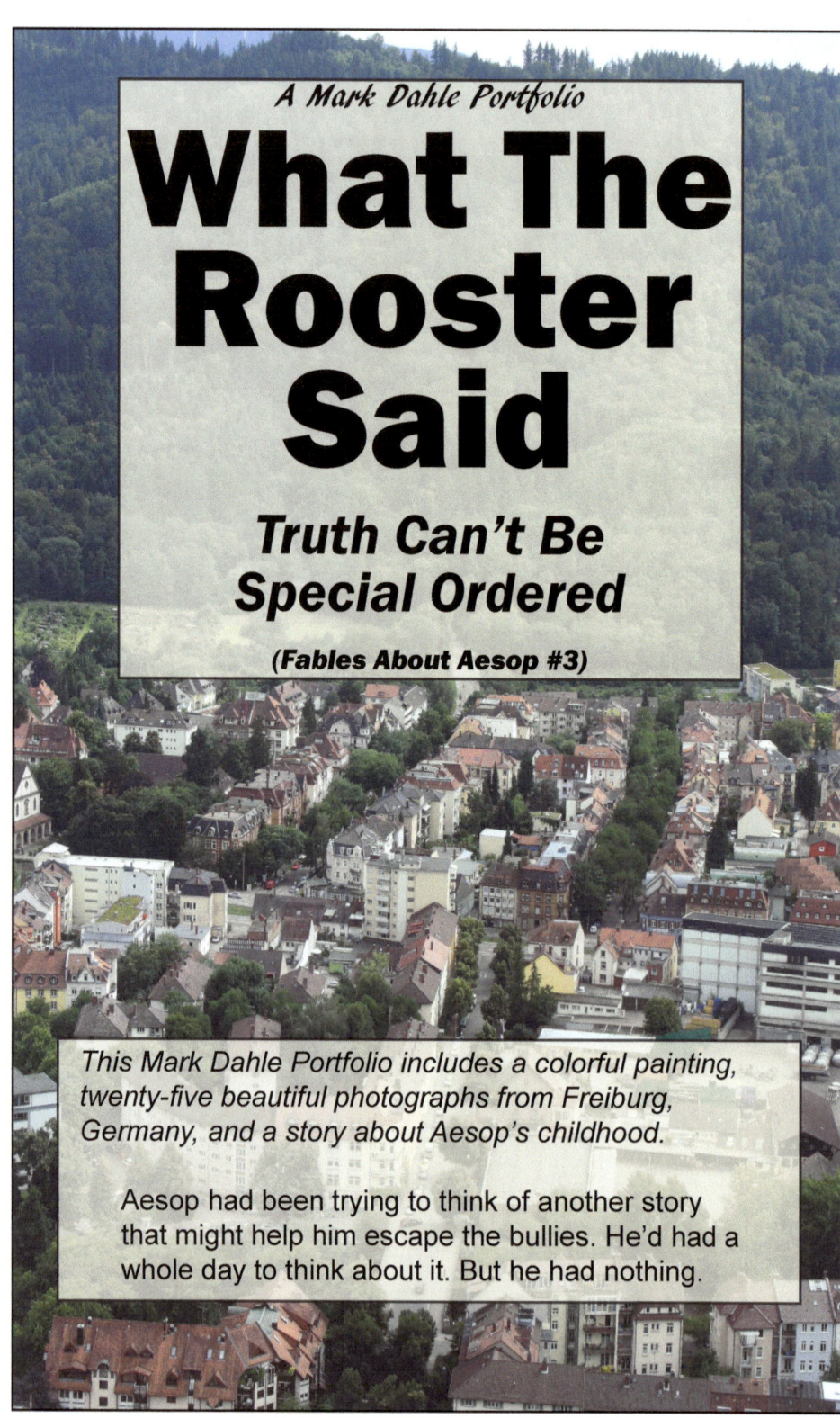

A Mark Dahle Portfolio

What The Rooster Said

Truth Can't Be Special Ordered

(Fables About Aesop #3)

This Mark Dahle Portfolio includes a colorful painting, twenty-five beautiful photographs from Freiburg, Germany, and a story about Aesop's childhood.

Aesop had been trying to think of another story that might help him escape the bullies. He'd had a whole day to think about it. But he had nothing.

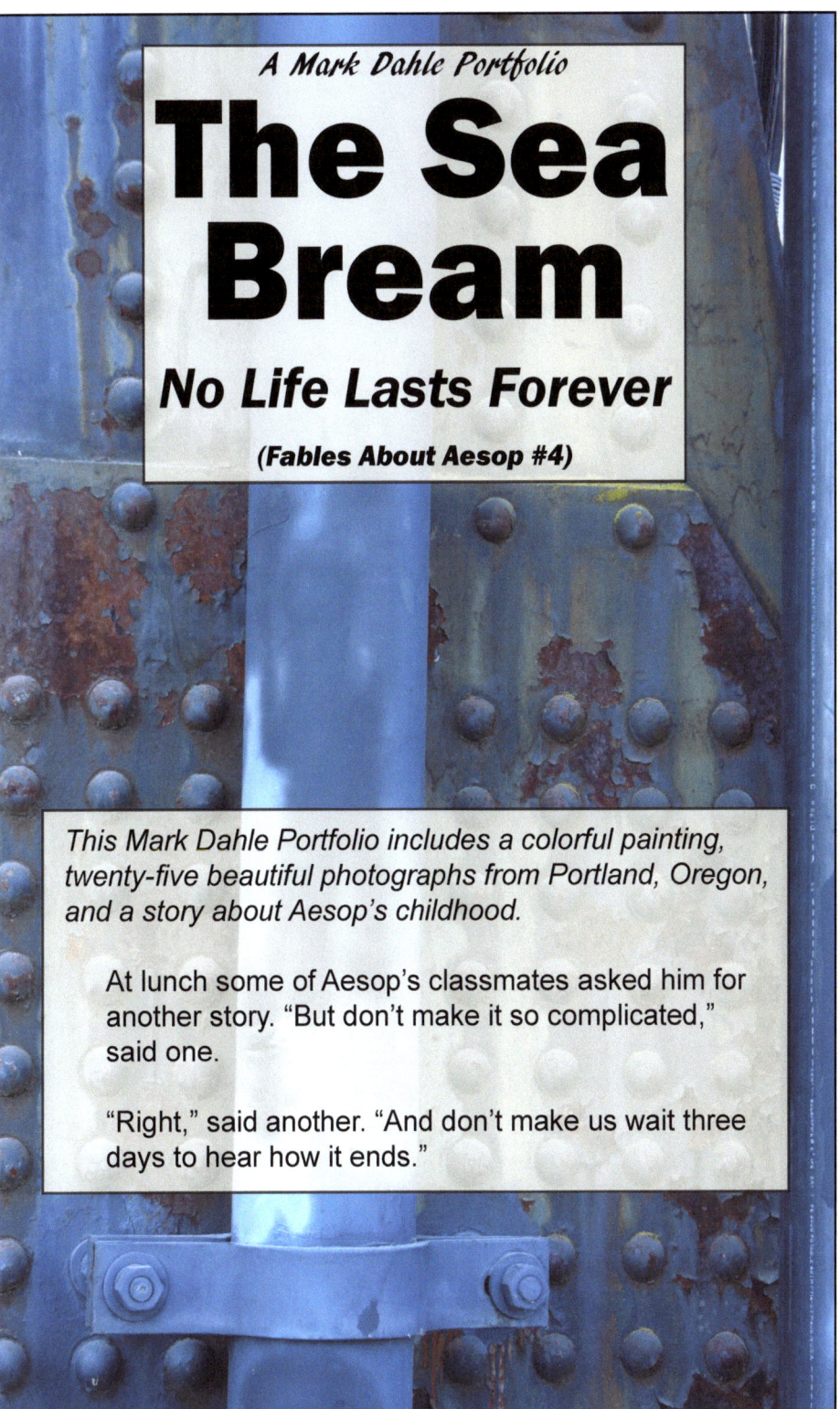

A Mark Dahle Portfolio

The Sea Bream

No Life Lasts Forever

(Fables About Aesop #4)

This Mark Dahle Portfolio includes a colorful painting, twenty-five beautiful photographs from Portland, Oregon, and a story about Aesop's childhood.

At lunch some of Aesop's classmates asked him for another story. "But don't make it so complicated," said one.

"Right," said another. "And don't make us wait three days to hear how it ends."

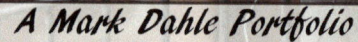

A Mark Dahle Portfolio

Tad And The Frogs

Friends Can Be Found In Unusual Places

(Fables About Aesop #5)

This Mark Dahle Portfolio includes a colorful painting, twenty-five beautiful photographs from Freiburg, Germany and Hawaii, and a story about Aesop making some unusual friends.

Octavia held Tad's shirt. Tad had written "I'm with Aesop" in big letters on the front.

"What does *that* mean?" she asked.

www.ingramcontent.com/pod-product-compliance
Lightning Source LLC
Chambersburg PA
CBHW040856180526
45159CB00001B/442